Praise for *WG's Birthday Party*:

'With amazing artistry David Kynaston manages to give us a social history of England while telling the story of this exciting match . . . *WG's Birthday Party* is bound to become a cricketing classic'

Guardian

'His re-creation of the play is as vivid as you could hope for, and he explores the past and subsequent fortunes, not only of Grace but of all the cricketers involved'

Sunday Times

'Charmingly written . . . As the match reaches its tense conclusion, one can almost see the Lord's of the old photographs, and hear the clamour of the crowd'

Daily Telegraph

'A pleasant book . . . You will finish it and think "What a period it was; what a game it was; what fellows they were!"'

The Times

'Most readable . . . Kynaston's book is worthy of such a match, being a fascinating story, well-told'

Journal of the Cricket Society

'Immaculately arranged . . . the events of the match, biographical details of the players, and the path they followed to the grave . . . An outstanding reconstruction'

John Arlott, *Wisden Cricketers' Almanack*

WG's BIRTHDAY PARTY

DAVID KYNASTON

BLOOMSBURY
LONDON · BERLIN · NEW YORK

This edition published 2010

Copyright © 1990 by David Kynaston

First published in Great Britain 1990 by Chatto & Windus Ltd
Centenary edition published by Night Watchman Books 1998

Bloomsbury Publishing Plc
36 Soho Square
London W1D 3QY

www.bloomsbury.com

Bloomsbury Publishing, London, New York and Berlin

A CIP catalogue record for this book is available from the British Library

ISBN 978 1 4088 1011 8

10 9 8 7 6 5 4 3 2 1
Typeset by Hewer Text UK Ltd, Edinburgh
Printed in Great Britain by Clays Ltd, St Ives plc

Mixed Sources
Product group from well-managed
forests and other controlled sources
www.fsc.org Cert no. SGS-COC-2061
© 1996 Forest Stewardship Council
FSC

To the memory of Jim and Elizabeth Robbins

Contents

On a hot July morning in 1898 the cricketing world gathered at Lord's to pay homage to the greatest exponent of the game it had ever known. The occasion was Dr W. G. Grace's fiftieth birthday. Shortly after noon, to a volley of thunderous applause, he led out his team of Gentlemen to do battle against the Players: the historic annual contest between amateurs and professionals was about to begin. This moment, more than any other, was the apogee of cricket's Golden Age, a summation of artistry, colour and individuality crowned by one giant, indestructible force. This short book recreates something of the man, his epoch and three days of enthralling cricket, uniquely of its time yet timeless. The story begins three years earlier, in the season of WG's never to be forgotten Indian Summer.

I

The Old Man

IN THE EARLY summer of 1895 the nation united in appreciation of a sporting marvel in its midst. The unerring voice of
the Victorian middle class expressed a widely cherished hope:

> Unmatched, unchallengeable Best
>   At our best game! Requite him!
> For thirty years to hold first place,
> And still, unpassed, keep up the pace,
> Pleases a stout, sport-loving race.
> By Jove, 'Sir William Gilbert Grace'
>   Sounds splendid. *Punch* says – '*Knight him!*'

There was cause for such rhetoric, for in May that year, at
the age of forty-six, Dr W. G. Grace had not only completed a
hundred first-class hundreds, the first cricketer to do so, but had
also set another precedent by compiling a thousand runs during
the month. These were, by any standards, phenomenal achievements. In the event they failed to secure him a 'K', but did
earn him something more tangible. Several testimonial funds
were quickly initiated on his behalf and together they netted for
him the tidy sum of £9,073 8s 3d, worth some £¼ million in

today's values. The main fund, amounting to over £5,000, was a national shilling testimonial organised by the *Daily Telegraph*, whose editor, Sir Edward Lawson, forwarded the handsome cheque with some appropriately weighty words: 'The subscription, commencing amid the hearty good-will and approbation of all the manly and open-air-loving section of our community, has broadened and deepened during its extraordinary and unparalleled course, until it has become, by the variety and significance of the countless names included in it, an epitome of English life in all localities and latitudes.' And, seizing the historical moment, Sir Edward went on to describe the fund as 'a very notable and emphatic expression of the general love for those out-of-door sports and pursuits which – free from any element of cruelty, greed or coarseness – most and best develop our British traits of manliness, good temper, fair play, and the healthy training of mind and body'.

But of course, as Sir Edward acknowledged, it was cricket above all that was 'the great national game', with W. G. Grace as its 'most eminent, accepted and popular representative'. How cricket achieved this dominance – transformed from a game into a quasi-mystical institution – is one of the signal mysteries of the Victorian age, still only half understood. But the bare facts of its astonishingly rapid evolution are plain enough. In the mid-1860s, when WG came to youthful, almost instant prominence, cricket was a fairly primitive affair: overarm bowling had only just been legalised; MCC presided listlessly over a dull programme of matches at Lord's watched by small crowds; teams on most first-class grounds changed in tents; and wickets were usually dreadful, even dangerous, with long-stop a position of such run-saving importance that special long-stop averages were published at the end of each season. Then over the next thirty years came the manifest signs of 'progress', combining greater sophistication with greater uniformity. The pioneering use of the heavy roller to improve pitches, the introduction of boundaries, the codification by a revitalised MCC of the laws of the game, the increasing standardisation of dress (gone the turbans and billycocks, gone the spotted print shirts), the growth of international and county cricket, the development of large, well-appointed urban arenas to accommodate ever-larger crowds, the rise of numbingly detailed and highly statistical cricket reportage – all these things played a part as the game inexorably seeped into the national consciousness. 'If the London clerk is often slack in his employer's service,' *The Times* wanly noted in a leading article on the occasion of WG's remunerative rejuvenescence, 'he is pretty sure to be a master of the last information about batting averages and about the chances of the county championship.' A small but telling sign of the way the game was changing occurred towards the end of the 1886 season, when a new telegraph board was employed at Lord's, altering the batsman's total as he made each run. Fittingly the first run was clocked up by WG.

For an increasingly prosperous nation, with a wealth founded on the twin pillars of trade and finance, there was something uniquely satisfying about cricket, a game whose very essence was of steady accumulation. Yet in an age permeated by middle-class morality (if WG was the hero of the summer of 1895, then just as surely the incriminated Oscar Wilde was the anti-hero), there were other reasons for the Victorian love affair with the

game. As early as 1850, invited by the Wakefield Mechanics'
Institution Cricket Club to be a patron, Richard Cobden (the
apostle of free trade) replied gladly: 'It is a healthful, manly
recreation; and, if the game be played under judicious rules,
such as you have adopted, it is, in my opinion, the most innocent of all out-of-door amusements.' Manliness, team spirit,
discipline, all joined to a sense of fair play: over the ensuing
years, a series of propagandists and others drove home the positive connection, culminating in 1897 in Newbolt's imperishable
verses of Empire:

> The Gatling's jammed and the Colonel's dead,
> And the regiment blind with dust and smoke.
> The river of death has brimmed his banks,
> And England's far and Honour a name,
> But the voice of a schoolboy rallies the ranks:
> 'Play up! Play up! and play the game!'

Cricket was also valuable as social cement, in an age that saw
the rise of organised labour and politics beginning to be organised along class lines. In his bestselling *The Jubilee Book of Cricket*,
also written in 1897, Prince Ranjitsinhji (helped by the more
fluent pen of C. B. Fry) gave classic expression to this line of
thought:

Go to Lord's and analyse the crowd. There are all sorts and
conditions of men there round the ropes – bricklayers, bank
clerks, soldiers, postmen, and stockbrokers. And in the pavilion
are Q.C.s, artists, archdeacons, and leader-writers. Bad men,

good men, workers and idlers, are all there, and all at one in their keenness over the game. It is a commonplace that cricket brings the most opposite characters and the most diverse lives together. Anything that puts many very different kinds of people on a common ground must promote sympathy and kindly feelings.

Yet at a deeper, less articulated level, what gave cricket its peculiar place in the Victorian psyche was the sense that, in an era of encroaching industrialisation and enormous, not always welcome technological change, it alone was a game that offered continuity with the village greens and spacious countryside of an older, more 'innocent' England. Fry came as near as anyone to putting this feeling into words:

The game is full of fresh air and sunshine, internal as well as external. There is generous life in it, simplicity and strength, freedom and enthusiasm, such as prevailed before things in general became quite as complex and conventional as nowadays. One gets from cricket a dim glimpse of the youth of the world.

Taking stock often grimly of the nineteenth century ('Let us hush this cry of "Forward" till ten thousand years have gone', implored Tennyson not long before his death) and hurtling towards the unknown of the twentieth, the late Victorians found in cricket a balm that soothed many ills.

All of which preoccupations – ethical, social, spiritual – meant precisely nothing to WG, who probably thought that the phrase 'It's not cricket' was a curious way of describing rugby football. Instead he concentrated on the task in hand, namely scoring runs and taking wickets, which he did not only in profusion but also for longer than anyone else in cricket history. By the mid-1890s, after some thirty consecutive seasons of first-class cricket, his figures were gargantuan: almost 50,000 runs, some two and a half thousand wickets, and about 800 catches, all numbers that have to be roughly doubled for his totals in all cricket; over a hundred centuries, two centuries in a match three times; ten wickets in an innings twice, nine wickets three times; the double of a thousand runs and a hundred wickets in a season eight times. Two basic 'contextual' points need to be made: that his batting feats in his early, greatest years (1869 to 1876) broke the bounds of all contemporary probability, WG scoring 52 centuries in those eight seasons, at a time when the average first-class total of an entire side was barely 150; and secondly that, though a few younger individual batsmen and bowlers began to surpass him in performance during the 1880s, there was no one in the late nineteenth century who came remotely in sight of his career achievement, let alone his unique standing in the game. So many 'firsts' were his: first to do the double, first to score a triple century, first to score a century in his first match against Australia. If one accepts – as one should – that one can only judge a performer by his contemporaries, then WG indubitably was the nonpareil.

His personal background has entered the mythology of the game: the father a cricket-loving general practitioner on the outskirts of Bristol; the mother a formidable woman who schooled her children in the arts of the game and justly won herself a place in the Births and Deaths section of *Wisden Cricketers' Almanack*. But was WG really a 'doctor'? Yes, eventually, after twelve cricket-interrupted years at medical school and an MCC testimonial match that secured him a practice in Bristol. As to what sort of doctor, there has passed down an adequate supply of stories about his good works, though in 1895 the flurry of lucrative testimonials was too much for Max Beerbohm; and he drew what for him was a uniquely savage cartoon, showing WG in the foreground planting the *Telegraph*'s cheque into a pocket of his cricketing trousers, while in the background there passed the funeral procession of one of his neglected patients. The historical truth is impossible to determine, but it was a healthy corrective to the hagiography of that summer.

Even better known than that maternal cricketing academy in a West Gloucestershire orchard was the physical appearance of a one-time tall, slim, loose-limbed young man who soon grew out and thickened to become an unmistakable national monument. Conan Doyle (who knew WG well) would later write about his 'huge frame, swarthy features, bushy beard, and somewhat lumbering carriage', before going on in almost Holmesian fashion: 'In spite of his giant West-of-England build, there was, as it seemed to me, something of the gipsy in his colouring, his vitality, and his quick, dark eyes with their wary expression. The bright yellow and red cap which he loved to wear added to this Zingari effect.' The cap was an MCC one and almost invariably it perched, tiny and incongruous on his huge head, as he batted, bowled or fielded. But if that aspect was mildly unexpected, much more so was his voice which, with a strong West Country burr, was high, even squeaky, especially when he was excited – which on a cricket field he often was. Of course, it has often been wondered how he managed to keep such a huge frame going through an unprecedentedly long career, especially from the early 1890s, when he was well into his forties, weighed over eighteen stone and was becoming increasingly troubled by his knees. The answer must be willpower and native stamina, never better shown than during three days at Gravesend in May 1895 when, scoring 257 (last man out) and 73 not out against Kent, he was on the field throughout. Some have claimed, perhaps improbably, that he was careful with his diet; certain it is that, during luncheon intervals, he confined himself in terms of drink to a large Irish whiskey with Angostura bitters and soda. But whatever his regimen, such cricketing longevity was in great measure a triumph of mind over matter.

It was a mind of character rather than depth. In the oft-quoted words of an old friend, 'WG was just a great big schoolboy in everything he did.' There was indeed much of the overgrown schoolboy about him: the boisterousness, the enthusiasm, the love of practical jokes, the willingness to engage in argy-bargy, above all the supreme lack of self-consciousness. He also shared a schoolboy's dislike of soap and water: one wicket-keeper described his as the dirtiest neck he had ever kept behind, and WG himself expostulated, 'We Graces ain't no bloody water spaniels.' His attitude towards dress is best described as some- what 'careless'; while as for book-learning, he once remarked to a Gloucestershire colleague fond of reading a Greek play while waiting in the dressing room, 'How can you make runs, Bill, when you are always reading? I am never caught that way.' Indeed, his whole attitude towards cricket, as towards life, was profoundly non-analytical. At Cambridge one year some prominent cricketers were discussing how to deal with the break-backs of a particular bowler. When eventually they asked WG for his opinion, he simply replied, as if stating an unanswerable truth, 'I think you ought to put the bat against the ball.' Or again, when it came to teaching his own children how to play, he would just take a bat and say, 'This is the way to do it.'

Yet the schoolboy analogy has its limitations, for at the heart of WG's character there lay a dichotomy between a general kindliness, especially towards the young, and a strong streak of the autocrat, often rather arbitrary in disposition. 'How are you getting on? Are they looking after you properly?' he would call out at luncheon to a young player on the visiting side, or 'Glad you had that one and not me,' would be his invariable and effective words of consolation to one of his young players dismissed cheaply; but towards a Radical in politics, or an umpire who had given him out leg-before, or a member of the Gloucestershire committee who attempted to interfere in matters of selection, his resentment would be both sharp and unforgiving. Moreover, for all his schoolboy traits, it would be quite wrong to think that he ever allowed himself to be seen as a figure of fun. 'Except for his real friends,' Fry was to insist, 'WG had a formidable eye and a beetling brow', not to mention 'an Olympian dignity'. Plum Warner put it even better: 'He could enjoy a joke or a bit of chaff, but he was not to be adventured on by any ill-timed familiarities. His figure demanded respect, and he knew how to ensure it.' The first modern sportsman to be a 'superstar', he handled his novel position in English life with much instinctive shrewdness, the very quality that had won him fame in the first place.

Nevertheless, the great imponderable remains: was WG a cheat? Anecdotage alone points to a conviction. In 1878, against Surrey at Cheltenham, the ball, having been thrown from the outfield, caught in his shirt and he ran three extra runs before he was prevailed upon to stop. Four years later, in a test at the Oval and with the ball manifestly dead, an Australian batsman went down to pat the pitch only for WG to whip a bail off and secure his dismissal. In 1893 an umpire again yielded when a Notts batsman played a ball from WG down in front of him, courteously returned it to the bowler, and on appeal found himself having to take the long walk. There is no doubt that WG was a formidable, even intimidating presence on the field, talking non-stop and appealing almost as often, even though he usually fielded square of the wicket. Many umpires, moreover, were afraid to give him out, including one at Grimsby in 1876 when the great man was palpably leg-before having made only six. He went on to add a further 394 against the local twenty-two, attaining the highest score of his career in all cricket. Some were strong-minded, like the old Surrey wicket-keeper Ed Pooley. 'Which leg did it hit, Pooley, which leg did it hit?' cried WG running up the wicket to him. To which Pooley countered: 'Never mind which leg it hit; I've given you out and out you've got to go.' A notable set-to occurred at Old Trafford in 1896. The Lancashire captain, Archie MacLaren, dislodged a bail as he set off for a run and WG, first to notice it, immediately shouted, ' 'E's out, 'e's out, toss 'er up, toss 'er up, 'e's out, 'e's out!' MacLaren refused to go and WG, after confronting his recalcitrant opponent, eventually appealed to the umpire. 'Well, 'ow was it?' 'Not out,' said the umpire, and for the rest of the day WG had an attack of the sulks, making him an unbearable presence for foe and friend alike.

Yet it is hard not to feel that, rather than being a systematic or conscious 'cheat', WG was someone so passionately committed to the game, and his success in it, that at times he pushed the parameters of fair play beyond legitimate bounds. 'An artful old toad' was the verdict of the Somerset all-rounder Sammy Woods, and there is surely a core of truth in that more kindly judgement. Certainly no one could doubt the commitment. 'Looking at Mr Grace's playing,' stated the oldest member of MCC, Lord Charles Russell, on the occasion in 1879 at Lord's of the presentation to him in front of the Pavilion after the testimonial match, 'I am never able to tell whether that gentleman is playing a winning or a losing game. I have never seen the slightest lukewarmness or inertness in him in the field.' Typically, he always began outdoor practice during the bitter winds of March; while as captain he would forgive anything but slackness. He also had the inestimable gift of nervelessness. 'There is no such thing as a crisis in cricket, only the next ball,' was perhaps his most famous dictum; and it is said that the only time he was seen flustered at the crease was as he waited for the ball that might give him his hundredth hundred. Such a man would have known by the middle of his career that he was untouchable, and for some twenty-five years thereafter he played the game hard according to his own lights, which were usually but not always those of his contemporaries. Nice customs, as ever, curtsey to great kings.

But important though these things are, they tend unfairly to overshadow WG the daily, functioning cricketer whose burgeoning weight made him adopt a very different approach to that which he had originally employed. A dashing long field was transformed into a capacious point; a fast-medium slinger became a slow-medium purveyor of assorted wiles; and a fleet-footed, fast-scoring batsman evolved out of necessity into something more immobile and stolid. Such was his robust common sense, allied to seemingly ageless nerve, muscle and eye, that he was able to make and sustain these crucial transitions with relative ease.

WG's bowling from the 1870s was to his contemporaries a source of wonder tinged with amusement, and several in later years would recall his unique style. Lord Harris provided perhaps the most perceptive set piece:

> It was very difficult to take him off once he had got hold of the ball. It was 'Well, just one more over' or 'I'll have him in another over or two' when one suggested a change. The chief feature of his bowling was the excellent length which he persistently maintained, for there was very little break on the ball, just enough bias to bring the ball across from the legs to the wicket; not infrequently he bowled for catches at long-leg . . .
>
> The success of WG's bowling was largely due to his magnificent fielding to his own bowling. The moment he had delivered the ball he took so much ground to the left as to be himself an extra mid-off, and he never funked a return however hard and low it came . . . He had also the additional chance of the umpire making a mistake over an appeal for lbw. He crossed over to the

off so far and so quickly that he could not possibly see whether the ball would have hit the wicket, but he generally felt justified in appealing . . .

The suggestiveness of the passage is increased by the memories of C. K. Francis:

His delivery was certainly baulking. Bustling up to the wicket rapidly, his huge shoulders and elbows squared, both hands in front of his flowing beard and the ball thus concealed a good deal from view, which made it difficult for the batsman to detect where it was coming from, his MCC cap tending to dazzle the batsman's view than otherwise, bowling generally round the wicket, he followed up his bowling quickly towards the off side, usually having a field pretty straight on the on side behind him. By this manoeuvre, he unquestionably caught and bowled a good many opponents . . .

In other words, if he really did bowl round the wicket and then move sharply to the off, he hardly gave the umpire much of a view of the proceedings – and presumably made that unfortunate official all the more susceptible to his frequent appeals. Indeed, the psychological element looms large in most recollections. According to C. T. Studd (the England batsman who became a missionary in China and the Belgian Congo), 'he was always so cocksure he could get you out that you had to strengthen your own opinion that he wouldn't or couldn't or else be sort of hypnotised and diddled out'; while the Middlesex batsman P. J. de Paravicini bluntly maintained that though 'he had excellent command over the ball and was full of tricks', yet 'he was a bowler whom a batsman only needed to keep his head to'. All agreed with the Hon. R. H. Lyttelton (of a distinguished cricketing family and himself a shrewd writer on the game) that WG's bowling was a thing of guile rather than beauty:

> He had a most ungainly action, he stooped, his arm was not raised above his shoulder . . . He had not the slightest objection to being hit, and had a field wonderfully and fearfully placed. Indeed, so long was his arm, and so far outside the bowling wicket, that many balls appeared to be well outside the leg stump; and yet when the batsman slogged to leg but missed the ball, lbw was frequently the result . . . Grace, probably more than any other bowler that ever lived, bowled for catches at deep square-leg, and he pitched just the right ball for this – not quite a half-volley.

It was a fellow slow bowler, Digby Jephson, one of the last of the underarm 'lobsters', who offered the most vivid account of WG in bowling action. He recalled

> a few short shuffling strides, the arm a little above the shoulder, the right hand a shade in front of him, the curious rotary action before delivery, and the wonderful length. The hand is large and the ball is well concealed, and, as you face him, for he stands full-fronted to you, it seems to leave by the back door, as it were, that is, over the knuckle of the little finger.
>
> He does not seem to do very much, but some come a little higher, others a little lower, some a little faster, some slower; on the middle-leg is his favourite spot – two or three off the leg

stick with a square deep who is not asleep, then a straighter one
with 'a bit of top on it' – the batsman tries to push to leg – there
is a somewhat excited ' 's that?' and the would-be run-getter is
sauntering pavilionwards.

WG by the 1890s was not the bowling force he had been, but
most seasons a respectable number of batsmen still sauntered in
the desired direction.

Yet however effective his bowling, it was of course his batting
that made him the universally acknowledged champion. His
historical contribution to that most exacting art was famously
summed up by Ranji in 1897:

Before WG batsmen were of two kinds – a batsman played a
forward game or he played a back game. Each player, too, seems
to have made a speciality of some particular stroke ... What
WG did was to unite in his mighty self all the good points of
all the good players, and to make utility the criterion of style.
He founded the modern theory of batting by making forward
and back play of equal importance, relying neither on the one
nor the other, but on both ... He turned the old one-stringed
instrument into a many-chorded lyre. And, in addition, he made
his execution equal his invention. All of us now have the instrument, but we lack his execution ...

Ranji did not exaggerate: there has been no more important
influence in the history of batsmanship. But to know more
precisely what WG looked like at the crease, one turns to the
sharp eye of Conan Doyle:

He stood very clear of his wicket, bending his huge shoulders and presenting a very broad face of the bat towards the bowler. Then, as he saw the latter advance, he would slowly raise himself to his height, and draw back the blade of his bat, while his left toe would go upwards until only the heel of that foot remained upon the ground.

He gauged the pitch of the ball in an instant, and if he were doubtful played back rather than forward. Often he smothered a really dangerous length ball by a curious half-cock stroke to which he was partial. He took no risks, and in playing forward trailed the bottom of his bat along the grass as it advanced so as to guard against the shooter – a relic, no doubt, of his early days in the sixties . . .

Of special interest to jaundiced modern eyes is the point about the bat being drawn back (probably to stump height) as the bowler approached. Conan Doyle went on to emphasise WG's great strength at playing the good-length ball outside the off stump:

He would not disregard it, as is the modern habit. Stepping across the wicket while bending his great shoulders, he watched it closely as it rose, and patted it with an easy tap through the slips . . . Never with the edge of the bat but always with the true centre would he turn the ball groundwards . . . With incredible accuracy he would place it according to the fields, curving it off squarely if third man were not in his place or tapping it almost straight down upon the ground if short slip were standing wide of the wicket.

All concurred that he could play all the strokes, though he tended to keep the ball on the ground, but it was Fry who described another speciality, namely 'the stroke with which he hit the ball from outside the off stump round to square-leg'. Apparently, to achieve this remarkable feat, 'what WG did was to throw his left leg across the wicket to the off ball and treat it as if it were a ball to leg bowled to him from the direction of mid-off or extra cover'. Few, however, would pretend in later years that he had been a Nijinsky among batsmen. 'Of elegance and absence of effort there was none', wrote R. H. Lyttelton, and Canon Edward Lyttelton agreed, though qualifying his aesthetic criticism with the dictates of utility:

> The style was unattractive, not because it was laborious, but because the movements were ungainly. The immense shoulders were put into the stroke more obviously than the wrists, and this took away all grace from the movement, but the power was astonishing because of the perfection of the timing and the leg work. For instance, in the digging stroke past point, what was noticed was the awkward heave of the shoulders as he bent right over the ball, and the curious prod with the elbows; but the force with which the ball went was astonishing, till one noticed that the movement of the upper part of the body was perfectly combined with a stamp of the right foot.

There is little doubt that by the 1890s a heavy-footed, crease-bound WG was finding the quick men easier to play. In 1896 there occurred the legendary innings in which the Australian fast bowler Ernest Jones slipped one through his beard ('Whatever are ye at?' 'Sorry, doctor, she slipped') and generally left him in a battered and bruised state. A friend asked him how he had withstood such punishment, to which WG replied: 'Well, he did rap me a bit sharp, but I don't mind even now how fast they bowl to me; it's the slow ones I don't like, I can't get at them as I used to.' It was only a relative weakness, however, and by this time WG knew enough about slow bowling (in the pre-googly age) to play it almost from memory. The last word on his batting goes to that prominent man of letters and folklorist, Andrew Lang, writing in 1893:

> There is something monumental in his stance at the wicket, wholly free from a false refinement, without extraneous elegancies. His is a nervous, sinewy, English style, like that of Fielding. Better graced cricketers we may have seen, such as Mr Edward Lyttelton, Mr Charles Studd, Mr A. G. Steel, all of them, in their day, models of classical dexterity and refinement. But it is always, or almost always, Dr W. G. Grace's day: his play is unhasting, unresting like the action of some great natural law.

Some great natural law . . . So it felt to his legion of admirers, confirmed for all time two years later when he broke all existing records as well as the hearts of yet another generation of bowlers. Often coupled with William Gladstone as one of the two best-known men in England, WG enjoyed a popular appeal that transcended class. If there was trouble in the ring at

Lord's, he would come over and, in Ashley-Cooper's words, 'put matters right with some well-chosen words and, often as not, a few handshakes with admiring strangers'; while in a very different ring at Haileybury School, a future prime minister (the young Clem Attlee) and his schoolfellows firmly held that, in the religion that was cricket, WG stood next to the Deity. It no doubt helped that WG was not a grandee by background and could be identified with in some measure by most elements of society; though as to what part of his lustre lay in his stagger- ing achievements and what part in his compelling presence it is impossible to say. That cricket in its coming of age needed a supreme representative is a truism, but that it found one of such outsize properties is surely one of the more acceptable accidents of history.

It was hardly surprising therefore that when in July 1897 this 'part of the national baggage' (the apposite phrase is Shane Leslie's) entered his fiftieth year, thoughts began to turn to how best to mark the approaching jubilee. That autumn the *Sportsman* put forward a suggestion, quickly seen by the cricket- ing community as entirely fitting: namely, that the annual match at Lord's between Gentlemen and Players, usually held in the second week of July, should the following summer be put back by a few days so that it could begin on Monday the 18th, WG's fiftieth birthday. At the annual meeting in December of the county cricket secretaries this was unanimously agreed upon, with the added provision that the rest of the first-class fixture list would be kept almost entirely clear so that the MCC committee would have the freest possible hand when it came to choosing the two teams. The Victorian public had long called WG 'The

Old Man', years before he was, even in cricketing terms: such was the deep-felt satisfaction in the continuing 'miracle' of his preservation as a top-flight performer. Now he really would be two score and ten, and the celebrations could begin in earnest.

2

Gentlemen and Players

GENTLEMEN VERSUS PLAYERS at Lord's was peculiarly WG's fixture and there could not have been a happier thought as the setting for his birthday party. It had also become a great and historic contest in its own right. Indeed, at a time when test matches were relatively infrequent and not necessarily representative affairs (by July 1898 fewer than sixty in all had been played), the annual encounter at the centre of cricket between the cream of the amateurs and the professionals was generally viewed as not only the match of the season, but also the sternest possible test of talent and temperament. If it lacked some of the social frisson of the Varsity match and Eton against Harrow, as a cricketing occasion it was unrivalled. The fixture also took place on an annual basis at the Oval, and sometimes also at festival grounds, but few if any would have gainsaid *The Times* in 1891:

> It is to the Lord's match that cricketers look for the crucial test between Gentlemen and Players. There is an air of importance about the fixture at headquarters by which even the cricketing public are affected. They know the depth of the influence possessed by the Marylebone Club, in whose hands the

representative nature of the match reaches a thoroughness that
can scarcely be equalled elsewhere.

The cricketers themselves relished the occasion and were
always, and in the most positive way, thoroughly on their
mettle, as C. B. Fry was to write on the eve of the game in 1898:

> Small wonder WG likes the match. It is the best one played,
> being in the true sense of the words a cricket match; a pure trial
> of skill, free alike from spoil-sport considerations of gate-money
> and from the artificial interest of the County Championship.

Yet for many years from 1819, when the fixture became a
regular one at Lord's, a basic inequality characterised the contest:
the Players, in short, were far superior to the Gentlemen. This
was particularly distressing because the underlying purpose of
the match (as with cricket generally in the first half of the nineteenth century) was as a vehicle for betting, and a one-horse race
avails no one. All sorts of contrivances were introduced to equal-
ise matters, culminating in the notorious 'Barn Door Match'
of 1837. The idea was that the Players would have to defend
four stumps, each nine inches taller than usual; and according to
Bell's Life, the 'novel match drew together a vast assemblage of
spectators, there being at one time upwards of 3,000 persons on
the ground'. The Gentlemen batted first on a wicket that was
about par for the period and mustered 54. When the Players
replied 'the monster wickets excited much attention', and they
struggled to 99, the great Fuller Pilch being out 'hat knocked
on wicket'. Whereupon the Gentlemen were skittled out for

a miserable 35 – Roger Kynaston, a future Secretary of MCC, top scoring with eight – and lost by an innings. A fortnight later there took place a return match at Lord's: this time the Gentlemen utilised sixteen men, but their two innings still only produced 116 runs, and again the Players only needed to bat once. Just occasionally the tables were turned, as in 1842 when 'the ground was most numerously and fashionably attended on each day'. The key figure was the Gentlemen's Alfred Mynn, who after battling pluckily on the first day for 21 'was in so much pain on Monday night from the injury he received in the leg from a ball by Redgate, that a dozen leeches were applied to the part, which reduced the swelling, and enabled him to go through the second innings'. Eventually the Players needed 163 to win, but Mynn, 'The Lion of Kent', undid them with his fast round-arm. It was the first time in twenty years that the Gentlemen had won without receiving odds. For some years thereafter it became a more even contest, but in the 1850s the old monotony returned and the Players won every year from 1854 to 1864. In that last year the margin was an innings and 68 runs, and not even the presence of two reverends could help the Gentlemen.

Then came a lanky, as yet unbearded sixteen-year-old from the West Country. His first appearance in the fixture at Lord's was on 10 July 1865. The report in *Bell's Life* is a reminder that middle-class morality had not yet laid its heavy hand on the game: 'Bearing in mind that the elections were going on at the same time, a very fair attendance mustered each day. The Players were the favourites in the betting, 2 to 1 being freely laid on them.' WG bowled the first ball of the match and, although 'badly run out' for three in his first innings while batting with his brother E. M., again took centre stage as the Gentlemen needed 75 on the second afternoon. 'The Messrs Grace began the hitting, and really brilliant hitting, too, completely bringing down the house.' WG himself was first out at 57, caught at long leg for a rapid 34 (including two fives), but the runs were hit off in fifty minutes for the loss of two wickets. The outcome signalled one of the most abrupt and complete sea-changes in the history of any sporting fixture, for over the next nineteen years the Gentlemen won fifteen times, the Players twice, and two matches were drawn. During this sequence, WG unfolded a succession of stunning batting performances, including centuries in 1868 (134 not out in a total of 201, on an unprepared wicket), 1870, 1872, 1873, 1875 and 1876. Unlike any amateur before him, he mastered time and again the very best of the professional bowling, ranging from the expresses of Fred Morley, the leading fast bowler of the day, to the sheer unrelenting persistence of Alfred Shaw, perhaps the last major bowler to rely solely on medium-slow line and length, knowing that the wicket would do the rest for him. Of course WG received help from other amateurs, not least from his brothers E. M. and G. F., but it is inconceivable that without him the balance of power could have been shifted, certainly not as dramatically and definitively as it was. The Yorkshire bowler Tom Emmett spoke for all the pros when he gave his considered verdict on the phenomenon that had risen up to strike them: 'He should be made to play with a littler bat.'

Eventually the pendulum swung again: between 1885 and 1897 the Gentlemen won only thrice, the Players seven times, and there were three draws. This was attributable partly to the rise of top-class professional batting, partly to the weakness in amateur bowling, and partly to WG no longer being quite his old force. But he played each year and in 1895, to general delight, he crowned that Indian Summer with a fine century on a fiery wicket. By this time, moreover, there had emerged a new generation of amateur batsmen, aggressive and accomplished stroke-makers who gave the Gentlemen's batting crowd appeal as well as new-found depth. In 1895 the great man's century was not quite enough, the Players winning by 32 runs; the following year the Gentlemen won by six wickets, WG scoring a half-century and taking a clutch of wickets; and in 1897 the Players won by 78 runs, despite WG's 66 in the second innings. It had become once again a finely-balanced contest, and not a few pointed out that it was due to be the turn of the Gentlemen in the historic year of 1898.

Such were events on the field in the nineteenth century between the amateurs and professionals; but meanwhile off it there had taken place an extraordinarily interesting power game, effectively resolved by the 1890s. The gist of what was a complex story was this. Between the 1840s and the 1860s the professional cricketer was, as never before or since, in control: the all-professional touring teams dominated the game, led by William Clarke's pioneering All-England Eleven, which spread cricket all over the country; they made their own arrangements, with MCC powerless to stop them; and the alternative structure of county cricket was still in its infancy. But from the mid-1860s (coinciding with the advent of WG) the touring elevens became badly affected by schism, largely on regional lines, and a more determined MCC began to acquire a firm grip on the game. Moreover, county cricket started to proliferate from the early 1870s, leaving the professionals with little alternative but to accept that as their main source of employment. A key part of the new dispensation was the stipulation from 1873 confining a cricketer to one county per season: the professional's mobility of labour was thus virtually ended and his dependence on the individual county became almost total. Further, within most counties a clear pattern of authority was now emerging: the local landed class provided the patron and, as often as not, the captain; administration tended to be in the hands of the middle class; a quota of amateurs (a mixture of upper and middle class) infused the team with the necessary amateur spirit; and the professionals were reduced to the role of hired artisans. In 1881 seven Nottinghamshire professionals went on strike in what can be seen as a last desperate throw on behalf of the fraternity as a whole. They demanded the right to organise their own matches, contracts that would be for the entire season, and a guaranteed benefit match after ten years of employment. The Notts committee stood firm, backed by MCC, and the men eventually gave in. The brief, mid-Victorian era of player power was conclusively over.

Thereafter the game settled down into a daily ritual of class-based apartheid. Its forms were manifold and pervasive. Almost invariably the amateurs and professionals changed in separate dressing rooms and came on to the field of play through separate gates – the professionals emerging from a side gate, the amateurs from the pavilion. The changing facilities for the professionals were often shabby, and *The Times* in March 1898, welcoming the attention given to players' comfort in the new pavilion at the Oval, referred to how 'the old professional box tacked on to the Pavilion at Lord's is always an eyesore to many of the Marylebone Club members'. At Old Trafford, where a new pavilion was built in 1895, three bathrooms were allocated for the amateurs, one for the professionals. At luncheon the two classes usually ate separately, while the apartheid extended fully to away matches: first- and third-class rail travel, separate hotels. Nor was that all. Amateurs called professionals simply by their surname, but the professionals would always say 'sir' or 'Mr'; and score cards and match reports followed hierarchical suit by printing the initials of the amateurs, but not those of the professionals. More informally, but still more visibly, there was even a separate sartorial code: the professional wore what had become standard cricketing outfit (all white, no great display of colour), but the amateur was often bedecked in an ostentatious cap and, off the field, a gaily striped blazer. There was, in fine, no mistaking the difference, as indeed there was not meant to be. Or to cite the deathless entry in the 1890 fixtures list, when a Leicestershire pro found himself in exalted company: Cambridge University versus Gentlemen of England, with Pougher.

But unfortunately for the smooth running of the system there was one snag: for though everyone knew that the difference between the two classes of cricketer was in essence one of social background, the trouble was that not all those naturally more comfortable on the amateur side of the divide could afford to obey the ordinance (as resolved by MCC in 1878) 'that no gentleman ought to make a profit by his services in the cricket field'. In other words, as first-class cricket became an increasingly full-time commitment, with an ever-fuller county and international programme, so it became very difficult for many amateurs to play in a sustained way solely for 'expenses', even allowing for a liberal definition of that often contentious term. The consequence of this was widespread 'shamateurism', a covert practice that could not help but fuel much rumour, ill-feeling and controversy. It was a practice that took many forms – gifts, testimonials, season tickets, salaries for pseudo-posts like 'assistant secretary', and suchlike – and has been well documented by historians. Keeping their amateurs sweet was a problem that preoccupied many county committees, and surviving minute books are full of ingenious devices.

Moreover, the greatest shamateur of the lot was WG. During the early part of his career he not only played on a paid basis for the United South of England (later the United England) Eleven, but in the 1870s also ran it on a profit-making basis, maximising his ability to attract large crowds willing to pay a shilling a head rather than the usual sixpence for the sake of watching him bat. When he went to Australia in 1873–4 his fee of £1,500 was a staggering ten times what each of the professionals earned for the tour. When he played for Gloucestershire he charged a minimum match fee of £20. In 1879 the MCC's testimonial match raised almost £1,500 for his medical practice. In 1891–2 he returned to Australia, charging the tour's patron, Lord Sheffield, the princely sum of £3,000 (again some ten times the going rate for a professional) as well as wide-ranging expenses for himself, his wife and two children, together with the cost of a locum. And of course in 1895 there was his amazing final windfall. Altogether it has been estimated that WG earned through cricket at least £120,000, which works out in present-day terms at well over £100,000 per season. Yet there was apparently no flicker of irony when *The Times* wrote in 1895 at the end of its leading article celebrating the rash of testimonials:

> We trust that the present movement will have the effect of making a provision which, when the inevitable day of his retirement arrives, will cause him not to regret that he sacrificed, during the years of his prime, his profession to the national game, and was content to be, instead of a busy country doctor, the greatest cricketer in the world.

It was not so much that he was paid – like most amateurs he could not afford not to have been – but rather that, though nominally an amateur, he insisted on being paid such an exorbitant amount. Interestingly, it was this blatancy of his shamateurism (or, to put it more unkindly, the sheer greed) that may well have been responsible for the distinctly double-edged feelings towards him on the part of cricket's establishment, no doubt added to the fact that he was hardly out of the top drawer. Thus, although the paramount cricketer of the day since the late 1860s, it was not until his tenth test, in 1888, that he was given the England captaincy; until the 1890s he was often passed over for the captaincy of the Gentlemen at Lord's; and he was never invited to be a member of the prestigious I Zingari club. Tactless, unwashed, seemingly impervious to the emerging code of 'fair play', WG was perhaps felt to be lacking in the necessary ambassadorial qualities.

If such were the establishment's misgivings they were clearly not shared by the general public, who saw no reason to question the implicit assumption that WG was a law unto himself and therefore entitled to set his own terms; while as far as shama- teurism as a whole was concerned, the popular attitude appears to have been that it was a reasonable price to pay for the dazzling sight of all those free-scoring batsmen. But what about the professionals proper, how did they feel about the whole set-up? By any objective criteria there were grounds for disgruntlement, since the lot of the average late-nineteenth-century pro was sometimes nasty, often brutish and undeniably short. Essentially he was casual labour, being paid per match, usually £5 at home, £6 away and £10 for a representative fixture. There was also a £1 win bonus and 'talent money' for good individual perform- ances. The richer counties might pay an end-of-season bonus, while from the mid-1890s they were introducing the concept of winter pay; a popular batsman might also benefit from the occasional ground collection. In all a regular member of a lead- ing county side might reckon to clear (after expenses) £120 in a year, which was appreciably more than a skilled artisan, let alone an agricultural labourer. But if – and it was the 'if' that preoc- cupied most professionals – he lost form or was injured, then those potential earnings simply vanished and there was usually nothing to replace them. Moreover, there was always the loom- ing question of the future. In theory the benefit was supposed to take care of that, but in practice it was a most capricious system. The county committee might not grant one; if it did it usually restricted the choice of match; and, to counter the ultimate nightmare of bad weather, most beneficiaries found it too expensive to take out insurance. In the event most benefits yielded three figures rather than four, and even the very best of the 1890s, the £2,000 received by Yorkshire's Bobby Peel in 1894, was paltry in comparison with WG's testimonials the following year. Many professionals doubtless hoped that, even if their benefit fared poorly, their career in the public eye would bring them something in the future. Ranji on their behalf was sanguine enough: 'A first-class cricketer, whose character is good, can rely with certainty upon obtaining on his retirement from county cricket a suitable and well-paid berth, which he will be capable of filling for many years.' Would that it had been so. Unfortunately the history of cricket's 'Golden Age', and indeed thereafter, is littered with sad, sad stories of human wreckage.

Most pros – poorly educated, often inarticulate – seem to have accepted their lot with a certain quiet fatalism. If they did grumble about being second-class citizens, or their uncertain prospects, we do not know about it. But there were exceptions, of whom the most notable was Nottinghamshire's Arthur Shrewsbury, the greatest professional batsman of the late-Victorian era. Shy and retiring in his personal life, he was also stubborn, clear-sighted and prepared to stand up to authority. In 1878 he was one of nine professionals who refused to turn out in a match against the Australians, complaining that the 'amateur' status of the Australians ill fitted their essentially mercenary purpose; and three years later he was, with Alfred Shaw, one of the ringleaders in the Notts strike. Early in his career he was struck by how often he played in matches in which he received £10 but an amateur netted £50, and over the years he not

only attacked the hypocrisy of the system but also strongly criticised MCC, which he saw as the great upholders of the arti-
ficial divide. There survive from the 1890s some snatches of
correspondence that offer a vivid glimpse into his feelings in
this whole area. When Shaw in 1891 was preparing to organise
Lord Sheffield's tour of Australia, Shrewsbury wrote to warn
him: 'I was told when in Australia the expenses of each amateur
member of Lord Harris's team was more than double those of
any one of the professionals'. A few months later, during the
tour, Shaw wrote to complain that the costs were far exceeding
Shrewsbury's estimate. Shrewsbury replied:

> I didn't know that Lord Sheffield had to pay for Grace's wife
> and family expenses in Australia. I thought he had repudiated
> that before leaving England. If he hadn't taken Grace out, Lord
> Sheffield would have been £3,000 better off at the end of the
> tour, and also had a better team. I told you what wine would
> be drunk by the Amateurs. Grace himself would drink enough
> to swim a ship.

The other extant letter was written in August 1894 to
George Lohmann, the marvellous Surrey professional all-
rounder, who was convalescing in South Africa. Shrewsbury
began by complaining bitterly that he and his fellow Notts
professional William Gunn had been planning to take a side
out to Australia (overseas tours were not yet under the auspices
of MCC), but had been thwarted by the Middlesex amateur
Andrew Stoddart, who was going to take a team out 'with
many amateurs who are hard up, and yet who continue to

get a nice round cheque each season out of cricket'. He then
provided some county news:

> Hear Mr Read is going to have a benefit and I should not
> be surprised if he got £1,000. Barnes will, if he is lucky, get
> between £300 and £400. The sooner you arrange about yours
> the better for you and the longer you delay the worse for you.

Barnes was another Notts pro, W. W. Read was a prominent
Surrey amateur doubling as that county's token assistant secretary, and Shrewsbury's estimates were just about correct.

Two years later Lohmann himself was the leading spirit in the
famous Oval strike of 1896. In the context of the decisive Third
Test, five of the professionals selected for England demanded in
advance that the Surrey committee pay them double the usual
match fee of £10. Bitterness over shamateurism and envy of
the money-making Australians both played a part, as did a feeling that some of the profits from the greatly increased attendances in recent years ought to go to the players themselves. The
committee declined to budge and three of the five (not including Lohmann) climbed down; but over the weekend before
the match there was much press talk about the immoral earnings of some of the leading amateurs, with the names of WG
and Stoddart freely mentioned. The upshot was that Stoddart
was too upset to play and that WG turned out only after the
Surrey club had issued a suitably disclaiming statement about
his expenses on these occasions. A distinctly huffy sentence in
WG's cricketing reminiscences, published a few years later, well
reflected his lingering pique: 'The incident was regrettable, not

only because the strike was ill-timed, but because it led to an unseemly controversy, in the course of which many irritating statements of an absolutely false character were made with regard to prominent amateur cricketers.' It was a pique partly caused by the knowledge that for once he had not been the popular hero; for on the first morning of the match, as the crowd waited for the rain to clear, the *Star* found that 'the talk round the ropes is all about the great strike' and that 'the voice of the people in this instance is unmistakably in favour of the professionals'. WG presumably found consolation in the match's outcome, England winning by 66 runs to clinch the series.

As for the day-to-day relationship between WG and the professionals with whom he played, the evidence is patchy and conflicting. Probably he could be a martinet on occasion, though at least one Gloucestershire pro would recall how he was a good friend to them. WG also had the justified reputation of doing his best to appear in benefit matches for professionals, knowing that this would add several thousand to the gate; and though more than happy to change in a different dressing room, he fully accepted that the role of the paid player was an indispensable one. 'Monkey' Hornby, the Lancashire captain, would have agreed. 'I wish to speak in the highest terms,' he wrote not long after giving up the position, 'of professional cricketers generally, who engage in a game of the most searching nature and, by their respectfulness and respectability, make their profession one for which there is much admiration.' Ranji struck a similar note in his *Jubilee Book*: 'There are few worthier fellows in the world than the average professional of the better class . . . He is simple, frank, and unaffected; a genuine person, with plenty of self-respect, and no desire to seem what he is not: on the whole, not a bad sort of man at all – quite the reverse.' There were, however, limits to the Prince's admiration, as a passage lamenting the lack of good amateur bowling made clear:

> High-class cricket nowadays is in danger of passing altogether into the hands of the professionals. Such a result would, in my judgement, be as bad for the game as if the reverse were to happen. Facts show that the majority of elevens composed entirely or even principally of professionals do not succeed. Judicious blends work much better. There is no doubt that, if the high standard of what may be called 'sportsmanship' is to be maintained, amateurs must continue to form a fair proportion of the entire body of first-class cricketers.

Two years earlier, interviewed in May 1895 by the *Strand Magazine* and 'with the kindly "burr" of the west country tongue lingering on every sentence', an even more eminent embodiment of amateur sportsmanship had already said as much. In the interview WG voiced his fear 'that cricket will be made too much of a business, like football – with the consequence that none but professionals will be seen playing'. And he added: 'That, I hope, will not come in our times; but there is that probability to be faced.'

Did the genuine dash and verve that many amateurs brought to the game justify these double standards? Possibly they did, art being long and life short; yet even at this distance of time it is difficult not to find some of the sententious hypocrisy mildly nauseating. What cannot be denied is that the rigid social stratification of late-Victorian cricket, reflecting society at large, gave a unique piquancy to the annual match at Lord's between those quaintly-named teams. 'All the Gentlemen should be players and all the Players gentlemen,' proclaimed Albert Craig, the self-styled 'Surrey Poet' and instant versifier of the contemporary sporting scene. Few would have quarrelled with these sentiments; and even fewer in 1898 would have wanted an end to the historic fixture. There was, after all, the small matter of a birthday party.

3

Cricketers All

B Y EARLY JULY thoughts turned to the coming clash, with the recently-founded weekly *Bat, Ball and Wheel* even running a special competition to see if any reader could guess correctly the composition of the two teams. The cricketing world especially began to focus its attention on WG, who so far in the season had been in fair rather than outstanding form. A week and a half before the great match he travelled to Leyton, where for the first time the 'upstart' county of Essex was being favoured by a visit from Gloucestershire. The stormy encounter has gone down in cricket history. WG began by taking seven for 44, including a successful claim for caught and bowled against Percy Perrin when almost everyone (including Gilbert Jessop at cover-point) was convinced that he had taken the ball on the first bounce. Perhaps the umpire was swayed by the triumphant high-pitched cry of 'Not bad for an old 'un!' Then, when Gloucestershire batted later in the day, the whirlwind fast bowler Charles Kortright took five cheap wickets but was unable to dislodge the Old Man, who stood firm for 126. The Essex second innings was again marred by poor, pressurised umpiring decisions, and the visitors were left with some batting towards the end of the second day. WG had made only six when he was caught and bowled by Walter Mead, but he refused to accept the umpire's decision and made him change it. The dénouement came in a three-ball sequence the next morning: off the first a thoroughly worked-up Kortright had WG transparently leg-before, but the umpire did not agree; the next WG snicked, but again the umpire turned the bowler down; the third uprooted WG's middle and leg stumps, making one of them do a complete somersault in the air. As WG stood unbelieving for a moment, his bat aloft, Kortright could not resist what would become an immortal remark: 'Surely you're not going, Doctor. There's one stump still standing.' Gloucestershire eventually scraped home by a single wicket, but a deeply aggrieved WG declared that he had never been so insulted in all his life.

That took place on Saturday the 9th. Two days later the MCC committee deferred its regular Monday meeting owing to the funeral that afternoon of I. D. Walker, a former Middlesex captain and doyen of Harrovian cricket. It was not until late on the Wednesday afternoon that the teams were finally announced. There were several surprises and none of the *Bat, Ball and Wheel* competitors had marked their cards correctly. Chosen to play for the Gentlemen were:

	Age	Appearances in G v P at Lord's
W. G. Grace (Gloucestershire)	49	33
F. S. Jackson (Yorkshire)	27	5
J. R. Mason (Kent)	24	3
S. M. J. Woods (Somerset)	30	7

C. L. Townsend (Gloucestershire)	21	0
A. C. MacLaren (Lancashire)	26	3
C. J. Kortright (Essex)	27	1
A. E. Stoddart (Middlesex)	35	10
G. MacGregor (Middlesex)	28	7
Captain E. G. Wynyard (Hampshire)	37	0
J. A. Dixon (Nottinghamshire)	37	6

WG had already played twenty-two times before any of the others had played in the match at Lord's, and indeed only Stoddart, Wynyard and Dixon had been alive when he had made his debut those many years ago in 1865.

The team included three specialist batsmen, of whom WG's likely opening partner was Andrew Stoddart, in every sense one of the most attractive cricketers of the day. Captain of Middlesex and on occasion England, 'Stoddy' (as all his friends knew him) was almost the complete batsman: attacking, graceful, spirited, with a penchant for jumping out to slow bowling. He was also a gifted rugby three-quarter who had played ten times for England and was capable of eluding almost any tackle. In appearance he was strikingly handsome, in character he was modest and kindly, and not surprisingly he enjoyed enormous popularity. Some of that popularity he used to make his way in the City of London as a stockbroker, a route followed by many Middlesex amateurs of his time and later. Yet if in many ways an epitome of the late-Victorian metropolitan sportsman, there were in Stoddart's case some important differences. His background was distinctly un-Middlesex, for he was born in South Shields and his father was a Durham colliery owner; and though educated privately in

St John's Wood, he did not go to public school or university. Moreover, he was an entirely self-made cricketer who did not start playing until he had come of age. But by 1886, at the age of twenty-three, he was batting through the day for Hampstead against the well-named Stoics and scoring a world record 485 – a feat made all the more remarkable by the fact that he had been up the whole night before playing poker. Seemingly still fresh after his monster innings, he followed it up with a lawn tennis foursome, a box at the theatre and a supper party. The real high point in Stoddart's career, however, came in 1894–5 when his team (as opposed to the mooted Shrewsbury-Gunn combo) toured Australia and engaged in one of the most thrilling, keenly-followed of all test series. At Melbourne circumstances dictated a slow 173, and he said afterwards, 'Well, I had to buck up for England, Home and Beauty.' To his own men he was an idol, coaxing and humouring the most recalcitrant to their best efforts; while according to the Australian player Frank Iredale, 'We looked upon him as the *beau ideal* of a skipper.' On his return he found a wax model of himself installed at Madame Tussaud's. But unfortunately, when he captained another team to Australia in 1897–8, it all turned sour: most of his side played below form and he himself was deeply upset by the death of his mother and the barracking against his team of some of the crowds. Altogether it was a miserable tour and seems to have affected Stoddart's love of the game, though in 1898 itself he was batting better than ever. Gentlemen and Players had rarely been a fixture in which he had shone, but he was an automatic choice.

'Heartiest congratulations. Wish I had seen it. Must have been ripping. Was rather anxious about my record though.' So

ran Stoddart's typically generous telegram in 1895 after Archie
MacLaren, batting for Lancashire at Taunton, had scored 424
and comprehensively passed WG's first-class record of 344,
made for MCC v Kent at Canterbury in 1876. MacLaren much
admired Stoddart and shared his commercial background, in
MacLaren's case his father having been a cotton merchant and
shipping agent in Manchester. There was enough family wealth
to send the young Archie to Harrow, but not enough to educate
the youngest four sons there; and afterwards, with university out
of the question for financial reasons, he tried banking and the
cotton business before settling down (or as much as he ever did)
as master at a prep school. Yet from the start of his cricketing
career he bore himself like an aristocrat; and when in 1894, at
the age of twenty-two, he became captain of Lancashire almost
by default, he accepted it as his right. Over the next few years
he made his batting reputation on the hard wickets of Australia,
twice touring there under Stoddart and in 1897–8 also deputising
for him as captain. MacLaren is still remembered as one of the
great autocrats of the crease, evoked in Altham's phrase about
his 'general air of proconsular authority' or the famous Cardus
snapshot of how 'he didn't merely hook the ball, he dismissed
it from his presence'. Cardus also much enjoyed quoting a story
told to him by Yorkshire's Ted Wainwright about a Gentlemen
and Players match, probably at Scarborough in 1897:

Mr MacLaren was on 49 and, as the match wasn't Lancashire
versus Yorkshire, I bowled him an easy one to leg, but he kicked
it away for one leg bye and came to my end and said, 'What's
the meaning of sending me that rubbish?' And I said, 'I was

giving you one for your fifty, sir,' and he said, proud like, 'I can
hit the *best* you can bowl, Wainwright, or anybody.'

Yet behind this arrogant presence at the crease lay a complex,
often misunderstood character, by no means to the taste of all
his contemporaries. 'Archie is very determined and always in
earnest,' wrote Fry at about the time of that retort, and he went
on: 'Does he lack humour? Well, he has a Scotch name. He is
very thorough.' Iredale in later years was more explicitly critical,
recalling how MacLaren could be 'rather brusque with strangers'
and 'had a sharp temper, and was rather impatient at times'. In
another set of memoirs, L. G. Wright recalled when he and the
other Derbyshire amateurs first encountered MacLaren at Old
Trafford in the 1890s: 'We found him crouching over the fire in
our dressing room. He appeared a glum and moody individual
and soon got up and went out of the room without speaking
to any of us.' But later he warmed up, perhaps literally: 'We
soon discovered he was one of the most delightful cricketers to
be with. He appeared somewhat pessimistic, but on listening
to his anecdotes one could not help feeling sympathetic, whilst
laughing heartily at tales told against himself.' Many of these
concerned backing horses and Archie 'would give his familiar
shrug of the shoulders and say, "Just my luck" '. Ranji summed
up the dichotomy: 'He is always cheerful and full of "go". He
imagines he is unlucky in everything, but Archie without his
grumbling would be like curry without chutney.' In July 1898
he did have a legitimate grumble about his complete lack of
first-class practice: teaching as usual had taken out the first two
months of the season, while the funeral of his great Harrovian

mentor, I. D. Walker, prevented him playing in the Roses match beginning on the 11th.

A member of the Gentlemen even more accustomed to command was the third specialist batsman (and occasional lob bowler), Captain 'Teddy' Wynyard. A career soldier who had won the DSO for his part in the Burmese Expedition, he was a man of many parts: in the Old Carthusian team that won the FA Cup in 1881; a prominent rugby and hockey player; an excellent figure skater; tobogganing champion of Europe in 1894; and recipient of the Humane Society's medal after rescuing a Swiss peasant from under the ice on the lake at Davos. But he won his greatest sporting renown on the cricket field, where his tall, athletic figure cut a fine dash, especially when he wore his polo-shaped I Zingari cap, balanced at the military angle with a strap under the chin. His other, less visible sartorial trait was a belt of flannel round his abdomen, which he insisted volubly to anyone who would listen was an equally efficacious protection against extreme heat and extreme cold. Having first played for Hampshire in 1878, he found his career much interrupted by military duties; but in 1894 his superb batting had much to do with the county achieving first-class status the following year. Soon afterwards he assumed the Hampshire captaincy and he also played for England in the decisive test of 1896. Quite the best description of the Wynyard of this time was given by Albert Knight, the Leicestershire professional batsman with a gift for the unexpected phrase. He looked back in 1906 on 'the greatest of all military players':

No English cricketer possessed more character, was more greatly gifted in the matter of strokes . . . In the quicker rhythm, the fiercer energy which distinguished him, whether, humming a tune and whistling an air, he flashed his bat like a sword from which runs glinted, or raced in mad career from boundary to boundary, one instinctively realised the presence of most brilliant capabilities. He had a wonderful stroke high and hard over cover, and a superb pull-drive to the on side from a ball a foot outside the off stump. This utter fearlessness, carried to a vicious excess, possessed him with an inordinate desire to achieve the virtually impossible . . .

Above all Wynyard was not a man to be crossed, for he was (in the words of J. C. Masterman, who played with him in later years) 'by nature an autocrat, supremely confident in his own judgement, a fierce competitor, and insistent on the full rigour of the game'. This rigour included the catering aspect, as a famous recent episode showed. Coming in to the pavilion after fielding against Sussex, he found to his wrath that part of a fine bunch of hot-house grapes, placed on the pavilion table specially for himself, had been innocently eaten by Ranji. Wynyard's language was so sulphurous that, in spite of Ranji's natural courtesy, a major row developed, Hampshire even threatening to cancel future fixtures with Sussex. Eventually peace was made through the good offices of Stoddart, who was due to take both men with him to Australia, though in the end Wynyard had to withdraw because of military calls. 'A good friend but an awesome enemy': the stress should perhaps lie on the second part of Masterman's verdict.

Altogether more colourless, but also more sympathetic, was Johnny Dixon, one of five all-rounders in the team in addition to WG. A reasonable medium-pace bowler, he was well described by Fry as 'a quiet, patient and sound batsman' and 'a thoughtful cricketer, with many ideas of his own'. His early career had not been without difficulties, for having made his debut for Nottinghamshire in 1882 he achieved little for several years, and indeed fared better playing soccer for Notts County, even representing England in 1885. Nerves probably caused his batting failures, but in 1887, summoned in an emergency to play for the county at Lord's, he scored 89 against high-class MCC bowling and thereafter played with a new confidence. In 1889 he took over the captaincy and for the next decade was, in Fry's words, 'regarded with great affection and respect by all Notts cricketers'. These included Arthur Shrewsbury, not always the easiest man to please. Dixon may not have been the most dynamic of captains, but this was more than offset by his kindly disposition, his entire lack of 'side', and perhaps also his relatively unassuming background, his father having been the founder of Dixon and Parker's, clothiers. In short, though few stories have come down about him, he was thoroughly well-respected in the cricket world, both locally and nationally.

There was no lack of stories about Samuel Moses James Woods, known to everyone as 'Sam' or 'Sammy'. The son of a Sydney merchant and blessed with the most magnificent physique, he came over to England as a schoolboy and attended Brighton College, making an immediate impact at both cricket and rugby. Dubbed 'the Father of Modern Wing Forward Play', he played thirteen times for England with the oval ball. Utterly

fearless at both games, he was hardly an adult before he had
become a legend. He made his debut for Somerset in 1886 at
the age of nineteen and his first ball, a fast yorker, produced a
brilliant leg-side stumping by A. E. Newton. His hard hitting as
well as fast bowling made him much in demand and in 1888 he
not only made his debut for the Gentlemen at Lord's (adding
much-needed firepower to their attack) but also played three
tests for the visiting Australians. He had also, after vain attempts
at banking and land surveying, gone up to Cambridge, where
he 'enjoyed every minute of four of the jolliest years I have
had in my life'. That was almost but not quite true: 'Little
Go', his preliminary examination, was purgatorial; and it was
said that all he could write on his papers was 'S. M. J. Woods.
Jesus', with even that having a spelling mistake. Otherwise it
was fun all the way, with bags of sport, a series of high jinks
and a unique reputation as an inspirational figure. In 1890, the
year of his captaincy, he breakfasted on seven hot lobsters and
great draughts of ale before going out to take ten wickets in an
innings; while the following season (back in the ranks after his
brush with the examiners) he won the Varsity match by pick-
ing up the first bat he saw, marching out gloveless and padless
and, in atrocious light, clubbing his first ball for four. Would the
rest of his life be an anti-climax? Woods subsequently described
his post-graduation policy: 'There is one thing I have steadily
tried to do: to drink more beer for the years I have lived than
any other man who has ever come down from Cambridge.'
He was not really so mindless – even at his fastest his bowling
employed much thought – but there is no doubt that he was the
ultimate warm-hearted extrovert. By 1894 he had thrown in his

lifetime's lot with Somerset, having been largely instrumental in their attaining first-class status, and he became captain and secretary for an annual salary of £200. Soon afterwards his pace began to fade somewhat and he felt his first rheumatic twinges; but he became an increasingly effective batsman, especially in tough situations. He also played three more tests, this time for England, when he toured South Africa in 1895–6. His approach as Somerset captain was summed up in his celebrated dictum that 'draws are only good for swimming in'. He had advice for other situations. 'If a batsman gets above himself, put one past his whiskers now and then' was one maxim; while as for batting, 'aim at mid-on's nut and you'll find the ball will go to the square-leg boundary'. Softly spoken with a winning smile, generous to a fault and as boundlessly optimistic as a Somerset captain of that era needed to be, there was only one Sammy Woods.

In a quite different way the same was also true of the almost too perfect Stanley Jackson, cricket's equivalent of Jane Austen: somehow beyond criticism. The reality was perhaps slightly different, but seemingly both cricket and life came to him with what lesser mortals must have found mortifying ease. Congratulated by a lady after scoring a half-century for Harrow against Eton, the young 'Jacker' replied, 'Yes, it is jolly, isn't it? Not so much for one's self, you know, but it will give the guv'nor such a lift!' The pater in question was a member of Lord Salisbury's Cabinet; while the family wealth that was to make Jackson one of the few genuine amateurs of the age derived from W. L. Jackson & Co, a large tanning and currying concern near Leeds. At Harrow he was a great 'swell', enjoying the confidence of the headmaster, Dr Welldon; and at Cambridge he was equally successful, captaining the side in 1892 and 1893. Amidst some controversy he decided in his first year not to give a place in the team to the manifestly gifted Ranji, probably through a mixture of racial prejudice and inherent mistrust of the young Indian's less than orthodox batting technique. Jackson himself, whether as an assured batsman on any sort of wicket or as a fast-medium bowler, was never other than supremely orthodox in his approach. By 1893 he was established in the Yorkshire side and also playing for England; the following season at Lord's he and Woods bowled unchanged in both innings to defeat the Players comprehensively. So the preordained pattern went on: in 1896 he was elected to Leeds Council and thus began his political career; the following summer he found himself captain of Yorkshire for much of the time in the absence of Lord Hawke. One should not be overly cynical, for 'Jacker' was not only a great cricketer but also a person of much integrity, if at times a little aloof. Ever immaculately turned out, he was well caught by Fry's sharp pen in 1897:

He always gives an impression of being all there, and having a very definite idea of what ought to be done and how to do it. Nothing excites him much; nothing can put him off his guard. Yet there is much enthusiasm for cricket behind those somewhat cold blue eyes and that unruffled brow.

There was, in short, no better man to have in one's corner when the going got rough.

Yet another all-rounder in the team who bowled fast-medium was Jack Mason, the highly popular captain of Kent. But batting was his forte, and more than anyone else he was in style the quintessence of the Golden Age amateur: coached on the true wickets of a public school (in his case Winchester) and essentially a tall, forward player, possessed of the most exquisite cover drive. He was, Altham later wrote, typical of that era of Kent cricket 'when Canterbury was all tents and strokes'. Becoming captain in 1898 only five years after his debut, he was thought by many in the county to be the finest, certainly the most elegant all-rounder since the time of Alfred Mynn. He was also a man of innate charm and modesty, nicely described by Ranji in his account of Stoddart's 1897–8 tour of Australia: ' "Jack" Mason is indeed a favourite among all. He does not say much, but a merry twinkle in his eye gives the idea that he thinks much, and knows much.' That tour was not an unmitigated success for him, though he took some marvellous catches at slip. Perhaps he lacked a certain inner steeliness; but few would ever deny that his cricket had a peculiarly attractive lustre.

Even taller and thinner, and quite as graceful a bat, was the left-handed Charles Townsend, who also bowled right-arm leg-breaks, sometimes of the very highest order. The son of the old Gloucestershire cricketer Frank Townsend, he was WG's godson and very much his protégé. In 1893 he played for the county while still a schoolboy at Clifton College and, in only his second first-class match, took a unique hat-trick, all three of the lemming-like Somerset victims being stumped. But the season that won him contemporary fame and even a modicum of immortality was 1895. Not only did he bat well (including partnering WG at the attainment of the hundredth hundred) but, starting in July, he began a remarkable run of 122 wickets in only eleven matches. Coming from an eighteen-year-old after long years dominated by the aridities of off-theory, medium-paced bowling to an offside field, these successes naturally caused much stir; and in the subsequent judicious verdict of Altham, 'on his form at this time he was probably as great a slow bowler as ever appeared'. During this magnificent spell he seems to have combined accuracy with considerable spin, and according to Jessop 'his pace through the air was too fast to allow of a batsman jumping out to him with any great hope of success'. Over the next two seasons his batting further improved but his bowling somewhat fell away, partly because of a type of 'tennis elbow', partly because he was overbowled by his godfather. Still very young and of a quiet temperament, Charlie Townsend perhaps failed to stand up for himself enough. But 1898 saw him in excellent form, with both bat and ball, and he well deserved his place. In WG's great match it was only fitting that the slim figure of 'WG's shadow', as he was sometimes called, should also be seen.

All good sides need an out-and-out fast bowler and the Gentlemen certainly had one in Charles Kortright. No one called him 'Charlie' and few to his face dared a 'Korty', though the word itself had passed into schoolboy slang for a really scorching delivery. Possibly the fastest bowler in all cricket history, he was also, in the apt phrase of Anthony Meredith, his best biographer, 'the most ungentlemanly gentleman the cricket field had yet seen': proud, aggressive, full of hatred for batsmen (especially if they dared show their disrespect by cocking up a toe), and perfectly prepared to hurt them. He was also singularly uncommunicative, preferring to let his bowling do the talking. Kortright's background was Essex gentry and he remained a countryman all his life; at Tonbridge School he was an unusual public schoolboy of the time in that he concentrated on bowling, traditionally the speciality of the lower orders; and subsequently he enjoyed sufficient private means to be able to despise the prevalent shamateurism. In the early 1890s he single-handedly transformed Essex's fortunes and made them into a county worthy of first-class status. Tales of his fearsome prowess began to spread, including the time at the Oval in 1892 when he yorked Billy Brockwell with a ball so hard that one of the bails flew back down the wicket over Kortright's head. In 1893 he burst upon the national stage and took nine wickets for the Gentlemen at Lord's. One was that of William Gunn, who said afterwards that the ball which bowled him was a yard faster than anything he had ever faced; another victim was Lancashire's Johnny Briggs, his leg stump sent flying some eighteen yards. The next year saw his county become first-class and during the first four seasons, 1894 to 1897, Kortright dominated the attack and terrorised many batsmen, even including Stanley Jackson on a sporting wicket at Huddersfield. Yet he was not asked back to play for the Gentlemen at Lord's – perhaps because his person-ality displeased, perhaps because his methods (often including a systematic use of the short-pitched delivery) were seen as unfair. By the 1898 season he was in his absolute prime and early on he wreaked havoc at Leyton against the Surrey batsmen. When there then appeared in the *Sportsman* a letter from 'A Veteran Cricketer' claiming that in this match 'the Essex fast bowler' (unnamed) had bowled dangerously short, Kortright at once replied. He refuted the charge and went on to cite the Surrey fast bowlers, 'neither of whom are proverbial for tossing them up too far', adding that one of them, Bill Lockwood, had given Kortright himself 'a very nasty blow'. This little spat clearly did not disturb him, for soon afterwards he entered a purple patch, taking between June the 25th and July the 9th, twenty-five wickets at nine runs each, culminating in the flying stumps of WG. His right to a place at Lord's was incontrovertible.

Charged with defusing Kortright's expresses with the inadequate wicket-keeping gloves of that era was the regular gentleman behind the timbers, Gregor MacGregor. Indeed, the catch with which 'Mac' had made his reputation in the fixture had been taken off Kortright five years earlier, low down on the off side while standing up. Long acknowledged as not only the finest amateur wicket-keeper since Alfred Lyttelton, but also as an outstanding rugby footballer for Scotland, MacGregor had learnt his cricket at Uppingham before coming to prominence at Cambridge. His great friend there was Sammy Woods and, sharing rooms opposite Jesus Common, they engaged in many an undergraduate lark, almost coming unstuck the night before a Varsity match when Woods threw a miraculously unscathed MacGregor through a plate-glass window. On as well as off the field MacGregor played the straight man to his boisterous friend, standing up to his fast bowling with the minimum of fuss, showing a seemingly telepathic understanding, and managing to be hit only once on his big toe. The two in tandem could be a breathtaking sight, and in 1890 his performances were rewarded with an England place at Lord's. When asked after the match how he liked keeping wicket to the professional bowlers, he replied that in comparison with his Cambridge captain they made his work very simple and pleasant, because they were so accurate. The following year he was captain, and it was his decision to finish the match in stygian gloom (and risk losing it) rather than go through the tedium of having to return the next day for a few minutes' cricket. From 1892 he was playing regularly for Middlesex and the following year he joined the Stock Exchange. 'Silent, determined, full of supreme self-confidence': Digby Jephson's description fairly evokes the rather dour MacGregor personality, though at times he could speak his mind plainly enough. Jephson also recalled him in cricketing action:

> He was always the same – even-tempered, imperturbable – at times perhaps bordering on the cynical; rarely if ever depressed by fear of disaster, or over-elated with the joy of success. He was a pessimist at the start of the day – he was an optimist all through it!

MacGregor might seem bored behind the stumps, but the appearance concealed unwavering concentration; and in the way that he never appealed unless he was morally certain that the batsman was out, he was the very model of the sporting amateur.

Such were the chosen Gentlemen. To modern eyes the obvious missing names are those of Ranji, Fry and Jessop; but as it happened Ranji was away in India for the entire summer, Fry was only in his first full season and not yet in prime touch, and

Jessop was out of health as well as form. Fry at the time was much disappointed by his omission, but took some consolation from Johnny Dixon, who told him that 'It takes a long time to become recognised in big cricket, and just as long to be dropped from it.' The press was more surprised by the absence of Somerset's stylish Lionel Palairet, and in his memoirs Sammy Woods recalled his feeling that Palairet should have been chosen instead of himself: 'Why I was played instead I don't know, though I suppose it was because it was WG's fiftieth birthday, and the committee wanted as many captains as possible to play.' If that indeed was their wish they achieved a pretty full hand, for out of the eleven no fewer than eight were county captains. According to the press, two of them were lucky to be included, namely Wynyard, who had played little cricket that year, and Dixon, who had scored only two half-centuries. 'One hardly thought he would be chosen', the *Daily Telegraph* said of Wynyard, though adding that 'no doubt his exceptionally good fielding has told in his favour'. While as for the Nottinghamshire man: 'Fine bat as he is on his best day, he is not half the man this year he was a twelve-month ago.' Nevertheless, it was seen as an exceptionally strong side, and more than one correspondent noted that each member (including even Kortright) had a first-class century to his name.

Could these Players match them?

	Age	Appearances in G v P at Lord's
Shrewsbury (Nottinghamshire)	42	14
Gunn (Nottinghamshire)	39	13

Abel (Surrey)	40	8
Storer (Derbyshire)	30	4
Lilley (Warwickshire)	30	0
Tunnicliffe (Yorkshire)	31	0
Brockwell (Surrey)	32	1
Lockwood (Surrey)	30	3
Haigh (Yorkshire)	27	0
Alec Hearne (Kent)	34	0
J. T. Hearne (Middlesex)	31	4
Reserve: Rhodes (Yorkshire)	20	0

Of the five chosen as specialist batsmen three were veterans of immense experience. None more so than the captain Arthur Shrewsbury, who as a twenty-year-old had first represented the Players way back in 1876. His opponents had included such names redolent of an earlier era as Lord Harris, 'Monkey' Hornby and WG's ill-fated younger brother Fred, who died four years later. Shrewsbury's background was rather different to those amateurs, his father being a draughtsman in a lace firm before becoming a publican. It was an upward ascent continued by the son, who combined a distinguished cricket career with not only running (in partnership with Alfred Shaw) a successful firm of cricket outfitters but also organising (again with Shaw) a series of sporting tours abroad, mostly in Australia. Throughout Shrewsbury paid the closest possible attention to his various business activities and his surviving correspondence stands as testimony to his sound commercial sense. But it was his batting that won him fame, above all between the mid-1880s and mid-1890s, when without doubt he was the best bat in the country, showing all would-be professionals that such a position was possible for an essentially self-made player. During these years he played some of the most celebrated innings of the era: 164 against Australia at Lord's in 1886, overcoming Spofforth on a rain-affected pitch in what Lord Harris many years later called 'the finest innings I ever saw'; in 1887 at Trent Bridge, a monumental, virtually chanceless 267 against Middlesex, compiled over ten and a quarter hours; in 1893 for the Players a brave, highly skilful 88 against Kortright, only a few days after he had been badly hit on the head by another fast bowler; and then almost immediately afterwards, against Australia at Lord's, an accomplished century on a difficult wicket, in the course of which he became the first batsman to score 1,000 runs in tests. Some of Shrewsbury's salient qualities were captured by Albert Knight:

> A dignity and a grace characterised the man and his cricket. He never hurried, never 'scrambled' for a run or runs. So fine was his wrist work, so perfect his back play, that the condition of the wicket scarcely concerned him. His expert timing, his faultless patience and unerring judgement were gifts which triumphed over ill-health, and made his batting at once a science and a style . . . He never compromised the grace and dignity of his method to satisfy a critical world unworthy of his skill.

Unrivalled on bad wickets, he more than anyone in the phase after WG's prime took the art of batsmanship a stage further. One secret was his confidence: if not out at lunchtime, he would invariably ask the dressing room attendant at Trent

Bridge to bring out a cup of tea at four o'clock. He was also, as Derbyshire's Levi Wright recalled, healthily phlegmatic about his cricket:

> In one match at Nottingham, Arthur Shrewsbury was given 'Not out' when caught at the wicket. Fortunately it did not turn out disastrously for us, but when talking to him afterwards Arthur said, 'My experience is that, during a season, the decisions given in your favour when you ought to be out, are just about balanced by those given against you when you ought to be in, so that personally it isn't worth bothering about.'

Yet there was a sadness about this small, pale-faced man with large ears sticking out from his head. He never married and lived for most of his life in a hotel; an intense wish for privacy concealed an essential kindness; he was phobic about his baldness and went to inordinate trouble (even in the dressing room) to prevent anyone seeing it; and he suffered from recurrent bouts of hypochondria. His fellow professionals respected and admired him, but few felt they knew him well.

One exception must have been William Gunn. Immensely tall and distinctly taciturn, he had played alongside Shrewsbury for many years and was reckoned by most judges to be second only to him among professional batsmen. Gunn was the younger man and took Shrewsbury as his great exemplar, following him by starting a sports equipment business. He also shared the master's empiricism at the crease, once remarking that 'I can make as big hits as anyone if I like, but if I begin to lift the ball I never score more than 40.' Together they shared in many long stands, usually against Sussex, and for hours at a time the cautious calls would be heard of 'No, stay back, Arthur' at one end and 'No, Billy!' at the other. During the 1880s Gunn flourished at both cricket and soccer, becoming a double international; in 1890 his 228 for the Players at Lord's was a record score against the Australians in England; and by 1891 his firm of Gunn & Moore was so prospering, in no small measure due to his industry, that he moved to The Park, Nottingham's most fashionable residential area. For someone who had escaped from childhood poverty only through being befriended by the great Notts cricketer Richard Daft, it was a remarkable story of self-advancement. Thereafter he was ever conscious of the often demeaned status of the professional cricketer, and in 1896 he was one of the Oval strikers who refused to back down. 'By this stage in his career he did not need the money,' his biographers assert, but 'what he did expect was proper recognition of his worth.' A world away from those richly characterful north country professionals beloved of cricket writers, Billy Gunn was the most unromantic and long-headed of men.

The third veteran, the Surrey opener Bobby Abel, was even smaller than Shrewsbury. Generally known as the 'Guv'nor' (though 'Bob' to his fellow professionals), he was not only an adored figure at the Oval but also a batsman whose idiosyncratic technique fascinated his contemporaries. Fry in one passage tried to encapsulate his appeal:

He gathers runs like blackberries everywhere he goes, and is very popular on that account, and on the principle of 'go to it, little 'un!' The average Cockney at the Oval suspects him of a

wealth of cunning – 'ikey' little dodges for outwitting the bowlers – and chuckles over all his strokes.

That was part of it, but not all. Crowds everywhere also loved
him because of his distinctive physique: many years later 'A
Country Vicar' would recall Abel's 'jaunty manner – his quaint,
bird-like appearance (a mingling of the roundness of a robin
with the self-assertion of a cock-sparrow) – his sidelong waddle
to and from the wicket'. Cricket lovers were also well aware of
how this almost toy-like man had overcome many disadvantages
in order to become one of the pre-eminent batsmen in England:
son of a Rotherhithe lamplighter; a parlous cricketing 'educa-
tion' on the rough terrain of Southwark Park; long, difficult
years of apprenticeship at the Oval; and in 1893, when seemingly well established, trouble with his eyes that almost ended
his career. Moreover, as almost all the more analytical observ-
ers of the game pointed out, Abel overcame these problems
in spite of employing a palpably cross-batted style. How? The
answer was a mixture of intense determination and concentration, quickness on his feet and a surprisingly long reach for one
so tiny. He also practised ceaselessly and looked after himself. Or
as Ranji put it in his *Jubilee Book*, for all his being 'a curious little
fellow with a slow, jerky gait and a serio-comic cast of countenance', yet 'he is all there – a tough nut to crack'. Coming
into WG's Jubilee match he was, as usual, near the top of the
batting averages. He had not, however, been enjoying a happy
time against genuine pace. At Leyton in May, Kortright's fourth
ball had had him caught at second slip for a duck; while shortly
before the teams for Lord's were selected, he had travelled down

to Portsmouth to face Hampshire's Christopher Heseltine (who had bagged him for a pair the previous year) and, in the graphic words of *Sporting Life*, had been 'caught at third man in trying to place the first ball, a full pitch, to leg'. Abel's place for the Players was unquestioned, but he might not have been hoping for a fast wicket.

The fourth specialist batsman, John Tunnicliffe, was at 6 feet 3 inches equal to Billy Gunn as the tallest county professional. Having first played for Yorkshire in 1891 he was now at his best. An aggressive batsman in his early years, he had settled down to play the more defensive counterfoil in a highly successful opening partnership with the stroke-making J. T. Brown. But what gave 'Long John o' Pudsey' his specialness was being in the vanguard of the eminently respectable – and socially deferential – type of professional cricketer starting to come to the fore, much encouraged by benevolent paternalists of the game like Lord Harris and Lord Hawke. He had attractive personal qualities ('a quiet, gentle manner, a low-pitched, homely voice, and the kindest of hearts', according to Fry) and his value in the Yorkshire team, notoriously a rough-edged collection, was considerable to Hawke. 'My right-hand man, the most loyal of all my loyal men . . . More thoughtful, wiser than the rest': his captain's subsequent tribute was heartfelt. Tunnicliffe was also a noted Nonconformist preacher and when on tour was usually to be found on Sunday occupying a local pulpit. In 1898 what probably caused his selection was not only his good batting form but Yorkshire's recent match against Middlesex at Lord's where, on that best of grounds to turn in a good performance, *Sporting Life* noted how 'Tunnicliffe again demonstrated that he is at present the best short slip in the country.'

The final specialist batsman was the distinctly undeferential William Storer, who though a fine wicket-keeper was picked for this match solely for his batting. In both capacities he possessed much ability: in 1893 he won national renown for the way he stood up to Kortright for part of the match between MCC and the Australians; three years later, at Derby against the formidable Yorkshire attack, he became the first professional to score two separate centuries in a match; and on Stoddart's unhappy Australian tour only MacLaren and Ranji batted better. He was also emerging as a quite skilful leg-break bowler. The fact was, however, that (in the tactful words of a subsequent obituary) Bill Storer 'was not an easy man to handle, and more than one Derbyshire captain had trouble with him'. None more so than S. H. Evershed at Leyton in 1895, when Storer originally refused to play after learning that his younger brother Harry had been omitted from the team. With play about to begin he had still not left his hotel; but the Essex captain agreed to a substitute wicket-keeper and eventually he turned up. Levi Wright tells the rest of the story:

Immediately Storer had taken his place behind the wicket he gave evidence that the 'madness' was still on him. It seemed as if he deliberately pulled his hands away from the ball and let it go for byes. Then, when Walter Sugg threw the ball in, he kicked it so that overthrows accrued. The spectators called out to him, and after he had kicked at one or two more throws in, Mr Evershed spoke to him and told him to play the game. Storer's answer was in accord with his temper and S.H. turned to me

with the remark 'What am I to do Wright?' I replied that there
was only one thing that could be done, and that was to send him
off, for the rest of us scarcely knew whether we stood on our
heads or on our heels. 'But think of his future' said Mr Evershed,
a remark to which I could give no reply. However, the game
continued. Storer gradually cooled down and subsequently kept
wicket brilliantly, making five catches in the match, whilst the
rest of us were quite disorganised and between us missed at least
as many.

His 'madness' also attended Storer down under in 1897–8. In
the First Test at Sydney, Australia's Charlie McLeod was yorked
by Tom Richardson off a no ball, but being deaf had failed to
hear the call and started walking away. Storer at once shouted
for the ball (which had gone down to third man) to be thrown
in, and on receiving it he pulled out a stump and appealed. The
umpire gave McLeod out; and although MacLaren, deputising
as captain for Stoddart, asked McLeod to return, he declined to
do so. Four tests later, also at Sydney, Storer was again a contro-
versial figure, this time allegedly saying to umpire Bannerman,
'You're a cheat and you know it.' The New South Wales
Cricket Association complained to Stoddart, and eventually
Storer was censured by MCC. But perhaps the obituary was
right: 'In spite of faults of temperament, he had a good heart,
and doubtless meant better than he did.'

There had been much speculation as to who would get
the gloves but, still suffering from a bad finger injury he had
sustained in the winter, Storer was willing enough to cede them
to 'Dick' Lilley. Probably on a par as keepers, the two men had

very different characters, Lilley being firmly in the Tunnicliffe mould and thus much more acceptable to the England selectors of the day. He had originally worked at Cadbury's in Bournville and learnt his cricket there when some of the foremen started a works team. Volunteering to keep wicket, and coached by an old Warwickshire pro paid for by George Cadbury, he made his debut for Warwickshire in 1888. Progress was steady, with bat as well as gloves, and in 1896, amidst some controversy, he replaced MacGregor for the Lord's test. He enjoyed a generally good series, and at Old Trafford even shed his pads to bowl a stand-breaking spell of legspin; while before the Oval test he predictably declined to join in the professionals' strike. Lilley was a safe, unflashy keeper and owed part of his success to the fact that, following advice from WG, he was a pioneer of systematically standing back to fast bowling. As he pragmatically told an interviewer from *Cricket* magazine in 1898: 'I don't think that there is anything to be gained by standing up. In my opinion you get more catches when you stand back, and it is very seldom that you can stump a man off a very fast bowler.' A decade into his first-class career, Lilley had cause to be satisfied: proprietor of the Oak Hotel at Selly Oak near Birmingham; one of the two leading professional wicket-keepers in the country; always smartly dressed; generally respected, not least for the accuracy with which he returned the ball to the bowler and his reputation for never trying to 'bounce' an umpire; and already starting to be renowned for his knowledge of the game and shrewdness of advice. Of this last characteristic Fry in due course had something sardonic to say: 'He was supposed to be a wonderful judge of cricket; but his main asset was a good crease-side manner and a wise look.' Perhaps so, but wise looks have taken men far further than 'Dick' Lilley ever went.

Among the Players, however, there was no more dedicated follower of fashion than Surrey's Billy Brockwell, one of the side's three all-rounders. According to his biographer, he was 'known for his immaculate attire, hat box and dandyism, and as a frequenter of London's theatres'. Indeed, he gloried sometimes in the soubriquet of 'Band-box Brockwell', though more often he was plain 'Brocky'. Sun-tanned, of soldierly bearing and often straw-hatted, he was a cricketer whom everyone seemed to like: crowds relished the aggressive batting that complemented his medium-fast bowling; fellow professionals appreciated his even temper and good cheer; Stoddart after taking him on his 1894–5 tour said that he hoped never to meet a better fellow or more pleasant companion; and Monty Noble on behalf of the Australians would look back upon him as a professional who would have made an excellent captain, for he 'indelibly impressed us by his broad outlook, his great ability and his charming personality'. In short, as Jephson put it, he was 'the admirable Crichton of his cricketing world'. Brockwell owed much to his happy childhood by Ham Common. His father was a blacksmith, his mother from a reasonably prosperous family of builders, and he was educated privately in the locality. In 1884 he started playing for the Ham club and two years later he made his debut for Surrey. It then took him eight seasons to establish himself in what was an extremely powerful team, but in 1894 he emerged as the player of the year. A rather disappointing tour of Australia followed – perhaps because he dissipated too many of his energies on writing up the tour for several papers and pursuing his hobby of photography – but by 1896 he had begun his very successful opening partnership with Bobby Abel. Having already done quite a lot of coaching in South Africa (and enjoyed an audience there with President Kruger), he went to India in the winter of 1897–8 to coach on behalf of the cricket-mad Maharajah of Patiala. Unfortunately he contracted malaria, but returned in the spring fully his usual, pleasantly assured self.

A similarly model professional, though rarely to be seen in the green room, was Alec Hearne. The son of 'old' George Hearne, groundsman at Catford Bridge, he was one of three brothers, all born at Ealing, who under the auspices of Lord Harris qualified by residence to play for Kent. They were all polite, serious in their approach to cricket and modest about their achievements. Harris was very proud of them and would recall how the eldest, George, was the first southern professional to take the field as well turned out as any amateur. Alec himself first played for Kent in 1884 as a leg-break bowler, turning to off spin after a few years in order to reduce the strain on his elbow; while over the years his batting, originally negligible, gradually improved, so that by the mid-1890s it was more consistent than his bowling. Never in the very top flight of cricketers, he was respected as a performer and much liked as a man, including for his quiet sense of humour. He was once batting against Kortright and, being quite a small man, had his cap knocked off. 'Oh yes, he's a bit fast,' he said afterwards, 'but he's not so dangerous as Mr Woods.'

Spearheading the Players' attack, and a good enough batsman to be classed as an all-rounder, was the sullen Bill Lockwood.

'He was never likeable,' later wrote the usually generous Sir Home Gordon, 'and there was in his bowling a viciousness somewhat characteristic of the bad-tempered fellow he always showed himself.' Albert Knight, in a passage born of painful experience, contrasted him eloquently with his long-time Surrey fast-bowling partner, Tom Richardson:

> He had nothing like the spirit of Richardson, succumbing to an unkind fate with far too ready a cynicism; but when the mood was his, and good or evil genius prompted, the sting and devil of his knuckle-raising deliveries was incomparable. Richardson would break back and bruise the batsman's thigh, apologising with grave and sincere smile; Lockwood would break back and nip a piece of one's thigh away, looking at one the while and wondering why the blind gods should waste so superb a delivery on mere flesh.

A bowler of moods indeed: Cardus reckoned that facing Lockwood was like dwelling on the slopes of Vesuvius, as slow-burning fires broke out without warning into consuming flame. Yet the man's life history was such that he had cause for a certain moodiness. Born near Nottingham in 1868 and a promising young cricketer, he found himself as an eighteen-year-old unable to secure a position with his native county after Notts had illicitly recruited Frank Shacklock from Derbyshire. Disillusioned, he moved to Surrey, where over the next few years he learnt much, especially about change of pace, from George Lohmann. The early 1890s saw him emerge as a great bowler, but then came a disastrous tour to Australia in 1894–5:

abject failure on the field and well-nigh catastrophe off it, as he badly damaged a shoulder, was attacked by a bursting soda siphon (resulting in a slashed hand), and nearly drowned during a pleasure cruise. There was much worse to come. Over the next two seasons Lockwood's form continued to slump and in 1896 he lost his wife and one of his two children. Then the demon drink took over, to such effect that in 1897 Surrey not only dropped him but threatened to terminate his contract. This shook Lockwood, who thereupon signed the pledge; but the Surrey committee was sufficiently mistrustful to send him in the spring of 1898 to stay with some Wiltshire friends of John Shuter, the former Surrey captain – in theory to give him some coaching but really to keep him under observation. Temperance worked, and over the following months Lockwood astonished the cricket world at large by returning to something near his very best form.

An altogether less problematic character was the ever-cheerful Schofield Haigh, one of that strain of happy-go-lucky cricketers running through Yorkshire history alongside the more solemn practitioners. He came from near Huddersfield and had spent three years playing for Aberdeen before being given a trial by his own county, making his first-class debut in 1895. Eight Australian wickets in an innings the following summer settled him in the Yorkshire team; and he was soon becoming a popular figure round the county grounds of England, with his rather slinging fast-medium bowling, enthusiastic fielding and capable batting at a pinch. He was a shortish man, loved practical jokes and was the devoted acolyte of George Hirst. Two of the sayings of 'Schof' would in time pass into cricket folklore.

One was his satisfied response after inspecting a sticky wicket: 'Methinks they'll deviate somewhat.' The other was prompted by coming out to bat and hearing one of the fielders say that the rabbits were starting. 'Oh, it's all right now,' he told the wicket-keeper, 'I've got th' key of th' rabbit hutch, and left the rabbits inside.' Haigh would probably not have expected his selection in the Players' team of 1898; but in the same match at Lord's where Tunnicliffe had distinguished himself at slip, played on a hard wicket, he had taken seven for 60 in Middlesex's first innings, including six clean bowled, mainly with yorkers.

The final member of the eleven was Jack Hearne, perhaps the ultimate professional bowler of the Golden Age. A cousin of Alec Hearne, he came from Chalfont St Giles, where his father was a carpenter and undertaker, and he was educated at the village school. Having been spotted by Middlesex's A. J. Webbe and qualified by residence, his big chance came in 1890 when he was summoned to Lord's at the last minute to play for the county against Nottinghamshire. 'JT' never forgot what happened when he got his chance near the end of the first day: 'I bowled J. A. Dixon with a real beauty, and as we left the field the great Arthur Shrewsbury said to me, "Well bowled, young 'un. If you bowl like that you will get someone else out tomorrow." ' Suitably inspired by these kind words, Hearne took five more wickets the next day. It was the turning-point of his life, and for much of the 1890s he proceeded to carry the Middlesex attack almost on his shoulders with his unfailingly accurate medium-fast off breaks. He never tired, never grumbled and, because he also never seemed to get sunburnt, was frequently referred to as the 'white slave', being indeed often the only professional in the Middlesex side. His greatest season was 1896, when he took 257 wickets at less than fifteen each. He was also by this time starting a regular coaching engagement in India (where he became a keen rider and shot), and it was at his suggestion that Brockwell took his place in 1897–8 when he was required by Stoddart in Australia. There he was the only bowler to show his true English form and he bowled many long spells. 'Apart from being a conscientious cricketer, he is a thorough gentleman in every sense,' wrote Ranji in his account of the tour, and none who knew him would have denied it.

One other name was on the list, and it was that of a young slow left-arm bowler from Yorkshire called Wilfred Rhodes, who would play if the fine weather broke before the match began. A year before he had been playing for the Scottish border town of Galashiels. He owed his place in the Yorkshire side to the enforced absence of Bobby Peel, who the previous season had been sent off by Lord Hawke for drunken behaviour and, reputedly, watering the Bramall Lane wicket in unorthodox fashion. It was an opportunity that Rhodes took with a vengeance, for by the week before the match he was top of the season's bowling averages, a quite remarkable achievement for a complete unknown. He more than anyone would have been watching the barometer with interest.

Inevitably the chosen eleven failed to satisfy everyone. Lancashire's J. T. Tyldesley and Albert Ward were regarded as unlucky omissions, as were Surrey's Tom Richardson and Tom Hayward; several papers questioned the selection of Gunn and Haigh, as well as the presence of Storer as a specialist batsman; while as for Alec Hearne, though 'doing so well this year that it would be ungracious to cavil at his being played', the *Daily News* added that 'there is no getting away from the fact that he often discounts his good qualities by dropping a catch.' Still, as the *Daily Telegraph* magnanimously summed up its discussion: 'Whatever differences of opinion may exist as to the sides, the match promises to excite unusual interest.'

Appointed to umpire it were W. A. J. West and Jim Phillips. They were a strong, well-known pair who in the Varsity match three years earlier had turned down all appeals against the light even though it had been possible from the pitch to see the gas-jets burning in the bar under the grandstand. They were both big men, and Bill West indeed had won greater fame as heavyweight champion of England in 1885 than he ever did playing cricket for Northamptonshire and Warwickshire. A man of modest and placid disposition, he seems to have been something of a side-kick to the red-haired Phillips, an itinerant Australian who, after an indifferent career with Middlesex as a slow-medium bowler, was emerging by the late 1890s as the world's leading umpire. He was much in demand in both hemispheres, and the previous winter had accompanied Stoddart's team, combining the demanding roles of umpire, general factotum to the captain, newspaper correspondent, and talent spotter for several English counties. Someone who admired him in his capacity with the white coat was Albert Knight, according to whom Phillips 'had that rare quality which admitted the possibility of error even when there was no alternative but to persist in its course'. And: 'He was reticent to a degree on the field, although none knew the rules or loved quietly to talk over them better than he.' Charles Burgess Fry, however, was less complimentary. After describing him as an 'elephantine' bowler, he went on: 'He was quite honest, but was ambitious to achieve the reputation of a "strong umpire". His other ambition was to qualify as a mining engineer, and he used to go about with a Hall and Knight's Algebra in his pocket.' There was a reason for Fry's disparaging tone. In 1898, fresh from having in the winter twice no-balled Ernest Jones for throwing, 'Dimboola Jim' was keen to stamp on any English transgressors; and Fry found himself the victim, being called in June first by West and then by Phillips himself. On the second occasion, at Hove, Fry according to *Sporting Life* was so 'completely disgusted' that he finished his over with lobs. With everyone anxious that the great match should not be marred by anything unseemly, it was perhaps another reason for his omission from the Gentlemen.

In the final few days leading up to the long-awaited Monday the 18th, the sporting press was awash with statistics about WG's career and tributes to his prowess and stamina, while *Punch* took the opportunity to celebrate with a full-page drawing. Meanwhile, on the field of play at Bristol, the man himself was continuing his splendid revival of form by taking twelve wickets against Somerset. All was apparent cause for celebration, but behind the scenes a major diplomatic manoeuvre was taking place: would it be possible to persuade Kortright, still furious about WG's behaviour at Leyton, to accept the invitation to play in the match in his honour? Eventually it was, thanks to the mediation of the great Essex amateur 'Bunny' Lucas, but Kortright travelled on Sunday to the Great Eastern Hotel, where he was putting up for the match, in a mood of pent-up resentment. Sunday itself was a day of broiling heat, though the barometer was falling slowly; and the London weather forecast for Monday was 'cloudy; some rain; possibly thunder; cooler'. But no matter what the skies might bring, the great day was at hand. One J. P. Kingston, a reader of the *Sportsman*, summed up the mood of the hour in some verses 'To W. G. Grace' that he now penned for that paper:

> Well done, Leviathan! we send thee here
>   A birthday greeting for thy jubilee;
> Unparalleled in scoring, now this year
>   Another half a hundred brings to thee.
> Straight as thy bat has been thy course in life
>   And still thy force unwasted forward plays;
> Thy splendid vigour with decay holds strife.
>   And Time, that runs out all, with thee delays;
> Thy fame has spread wherever bat and ball
>   Ring with their joyous clatter o'er the field.
> On this thy birthday may no shadows fall,
>   And may it still a further hundred yield;
> Thou art the centre of a million eyes
>   Who love our summer game and sunny skies.

4

Monday

THE BIRTHDAY DAWNED fair and from soon after breakfast all roads led to St John's Wood. Excursion trains were run from the west of England; travellers on the Metropolitan line were subject to vexing delays, with the rumour at Baker Street being that this was due to the early return to London of the Prince of Wales, who had hurt his knee while spending the weekend with the Rothschilds near Aylesbury; and everywhere there were hansom cabs, some of the horses collapsing under the heat and blocking the already crowded streets. Long before the gates were opened at half-past ten (with the match due to start at noon) a big crowd had collected outside the ground. The admirably unmercenary MCC charged its usual admission of sixpence and, as the turnstiles clicked away busily, all seats except those in the Pavilion were occupied within the hour. Rows six or seven deep of standing spectators formed behind the seats. The crush at what was meant to be the 'reserved' stand opposite the tavern was especially intense, and much to their annoyance people were being turned away from it in their hundreds. Long before play began every convenient vantage point had been taken, and the authorities made the sensible decision to allow some of the thousands still milling outside the ground to enter and squat as they could round the boundary edge.

The capacity at Lord's, severely stretched this day, was just over 20,000; but apart from the mock-Gothic Pavilion, built in 1890, the ground bore only a faint resemblance to the concreted stadium familiar in our own time. The few permanent stands that existed tended to be low; Block A (now the Warner Stand) was uncovered and made do on big match days with an improvised awning; the tavern was still a hotel; and farther along the south side, towards the largely undeveloped nursery end, the ivy-clad building containing the real tennis court added a gracious touch. In short, though the Lord's of 1898 may have been far removed in aspect from that 'tented field' it had been earlier in the century, it still as a whole presented a pleasingly unassuming appearance. As it happened, however, Gentlemen and Players was to be the last major occasion before a fundamental change; for at the club's AGM in May it had been decided, following undignified, even rowdy crowd scenes at the test match two years earlier, to pull down the tennis and racquets courts and two nearby houses on St John's Wood Road, build a new real tennis court at the back of the Pavilion, and construct a new stand in time for the 1899 season, when the Australians were coming again. Thus was born the Mound Stand, providing substantial additional accommodation; while an important result of these changes would be to throw back the line of seating along the south side by some ten to fifteen yards, helping to ensure more orderly proceedings. The knowledge that a historic intimacy would soon be lost added a certain pre-emptive nostalgia to this densely populous Monday morning.

WG himself, accompanied by his wife and daughter and no doubt wearing his favourite half-topper black hat, arrived at the ground a few minutes before eleven. Renowned for his bone-crushing grip, he found everyone over the next hour wanting to take the risk and shake him by the hand; and as he slowly made his way round the north side of the ground to the mobile post office, where some hundred telegrams of congratulation awaited him, he was greeted with hearty cheers and continuous shouts of 'many happy returns', and to one and all he smiled his expansive smile. For once WG found that he had no time for his usual morning net practice, but all the other cricketers went down to the nursery end and were watched by scores of spectators unable to get a seat in the ring round the playing area. Those with seats did not dare risk losing their places, but patiently waited for the clock on the outside of the tennis court to inch its way round to twelve.

Team news was that, with the weather still dry and the wicket hard, Rhodes remained reserve, which meant that there was to be no left-arm bowler in the match. As for the other great question, the toss, it was left in this pre-loudspeaker age for Albert Craig, the 'Surrey Poet', to inform the ring that, Shrewsbury having won it, the Players would bat. Popular reaction was mixed: some expressed satisfaction that they would get a good dose of WG in the field, others (especially those able to take only one day off work) were sorry they might not see the Old Man bat on his birthday. Where there was agreement, from press box in the grandstand to members in the Pavilion to cricket-lovers round the ground, was that on what was confidently expected to be a fast, true wicket there should be a packet of runs for

the side batting first. The Gentlemen, with their slightly weak
attack, seemed likely to have a long, hot day in front of them.

At noon a hush spread over Lord's and all eyes turned to
the doorway in the centre of the Pavilion. One minute, two
minutes went by, WG's face was briefly glimpsed by the door
but then vanished, perhaps as he waited for some of the strag-
glers in his team to make their way downstairs and through the
Long Room. At last, at three minutes past, the enormous, indestructible figure with greying beard and striped cap emerged
from the door and, followed at a respectful distance by his
colleagues, came down the Pavilion steps and through the gate.
Everyone on the ground stood and there rose a mighty, deafen-
ing, inarticulate roar, followed by a volley of hurrahs, gradually dwindling to a rattling small-fire of 'Good old Grace!' and
'Many happy returns!' WG responded to the acclaim with a
modest, half deprecatory salute in military fashion. A minute
later and another large cheer went up, this time as the diminu-
tive opening pair came through the professionals' side gate. Abel
wore his familiar faded chocolate-coloured cap, Shrewsbury a
white slouch hat; for the Nottinghamshire man too, who had
first captained the Players at Lord's back in 1885, this was a
culminating moment.

WG and Kortright were still not on speaking terms, but
between them they contrived to set a field for the demon's
opening over from the Pavilion end. And fearsomely attacking
it was too: MacGregor eschewing heroics and standing some
dozen yards back; Wynyard, Mason, Stoddart and MacLaren
in the slips alongside him; Dixon on the third-man boundary;
WG as ever at point; Jackson at cover; Townsend at mid-off;

and the bareheaded Woods at mid-on, the only man on the leg side. At five minutes past, WG's jubilee match began and, as the first ball whizzed past Shrewsbury, an audible 'whew' went all round the ring of spectators. The veteran gingerly survived the remaining four balls of the over. Jackson then bowled to Abel with a markedly less aggressive field and, with MacGregor standing up, almost got a stumping off the fifth and final ball of the over. Two more maidens followed before, off the last ball of Kortright's third over, Shrewsbury blocked one towards cover-point and, taking advantage of the Old Man's immobility, ran a quick single. The Players were at last under way.

During these opening exchanges Jackson bowled his easy-actioned fast-medium break-backs with admirable control, but all eyes were on Kortright, who seemed to be bowling faster than even he had ever bowled before. He was also pitching them short and getting plenty of lift, causing Shrewsbury palpable ill ease. There was nothing sophisticated about 'Korty' as a bowler – he simply bowled as fast as he possibly could and did not trouble himself about such faddish concerns as the use of the seam or swing through the air. Indeed, he would even rub the new ball in the dirt in order to obtain as firm a grip as possible for the sake of accuracy. He walked back some twenty paces, turned and then charged in with his arms working like piston rods. There was no slowing down as he reached the wicket; but instead it was all one rushing movement as, with a high, full-fronted sweeping action and bowling off his toes, he released the ball with great velocity. 1898 was the first season he had not sported a moustache and from the other end of the pitch this somehow added to the terrifying effect, accentuating his scowling dislike of all batsmen. This morning, inspired by the occasion and perhaps also by the wish to prove something to WG, he was letting himself go like a steam engine (as one observer graphically put it) and no batsman in the world would have relished the prospect.

Least of all the 'Guv'nor'. Over the next half hour he was quite unable to hide his fear and his right foot kept moving back towards square leg, usually followed by the bat and the rest of his body. Abel did manage an off-driven four to the covered stand from an overpitched one, but for all his studiously correct practice strokes between balls he was having a miserable time of it. Shrewsbury also remained unhappy and both men found their eyebrows uncomfortably close to several of Kortright's deliveries. With the score at 11, WG left the field perceptibly limping: a bruised heel had been giving him trouble for a week or two and he now went off for treatment. During his absence, in which Stoddart took over the captaincy and Tunnicliffe fielded as substitute, the batsmen continued on the defensive, bent on physical as well as cricketing survival. A ball from Kortright caught the shoulder of Shrewsbury's bat and just cleared Stoddart, and soon afterwards, to an anxious gasp from the crowd, he only just got his head out of the way of a bumper. Abel could not get either bowler away, two well-timed cuts off Kortright being smartly stopped by MacLaren, and what runs there were were mainly scored by Shrewsbury off Jackson. With three-quarters of an hour of play gone, and WG back in the fray, the score was only 25.

Under ideal conditions of brilliant sunshine and a pleasant tempering breeze, this rather brutal contest was being watched by a crowd of distinction as well as size, containing as it did many notable cricketers past and present. The majority of spectators were straw-hatted, but in the Pavilion the top hat was almost *de rigueur*. There were few ladies present, certainly in comparison with the Varsity match or Eton and Harrow; and all were somewhat complacently agreed that this was not a 'social picnic' occasion, but rather one for true and disinterested lovers of the game. From the start the cricket was scrutinised with intense concentration and also, once a tendency to applaud loudly every time the ball came near WG had died down, with much discrimination. Anything worthy of applause received a generous round, but something like derision greeted mishits, of which there were not a few in the early stages. Packed in like sardines, and seeing the action as best it could, the vast gathering was determined to relish everything.

Townsend with his leg-breaks now replaced Jackson at the nursery end and bowled a maiden to Shrewsbury, whose composure was sufficiently shaken for him to miss an easy chance to hit one to leg for four. Then it was Kortright again and to his first ball Abel, still suffering from a crack on the ribs a few minutes earlier, nervously shaped to play forward and was clean bowled leg stump, the ball perhaps keeping a fraction low. In an effort unworthy of the occasion he had scored 7 in fifty minutes. Abel was replaced by Gunn, who failed to lay a bat on any of the remaining four deliveries and came within a whisker of being bowled by an especially fast one. At the other end Shrewsbury was playing a typically watchful game, refusing to be tempted by a series of balls outside the off stump from Townsend, until at last he did essay a cut and was nicely caught at slip by Kortright, taking the ball almost as it passed him. For once Shrewsbury's patience had failed him and, as he himself ruefully remarked afterwards, he would not usually have been out from such a ball once in fifty times. An hour of play had gone and the rather dismal score was 29 for two.

It was at about this time or soon after that WG sought to end the silent feud. 'Well, Korty, want to change, want to go off?' he asked. A pause. 'Well, I can keep on,' was the gruff reply. So Kortright kept on, but gradually over the next half hour Gunn (with the advantage of his height) and Storer came to terms with his pace, which even he could not sustain unabated in the hot sun. One over cost him nine runs, including a good hit to leg by Storer and a fortuitous snick by Gunn. There were other moments of ill fortune for the bowler: first umpire West declined to uphold an appeal for caught behind against Storer, and then the same batsman was missed at slip by the usually reliable Wynyard; while in general the pattern of the first hour continued, with batsmen failing to get a touch and edges going tantalisingly close to hand. By half-past one, with the score on 66, WG at last decided that it was time to give his main strike bowler a rest, and Lord's echoed to richly deserved applause for his efforts.

It was as well for the Players that the combative Storer had been chosen as a specialist batsman, for coming in at something of a crisis, and bearing the full brunt of the Kortright onslaught, his pluck and his nerve were invaluable. By the time Kortright came off he was starting to play an innings full of vigour and robustness, allied to quick running between the wickets (befitting a former soccer player) that not only got the veteran Gunn moving but also generally quickened the tempo of the rather moribund Players' innings. No one would ever call Storer an elegant batsman, and he stood rather crouched at the crease; but he had a resolute defence and a particularly strong pull, the once-prohibited stroke that E. M. Grace had pioneered and WG had resolutely refused to play until after he was forty years of age and needed fresh weapons in his armoury to compensate for slowing footwork. He also had a special stroke, perhaps modelled on Ranji, in which he moved his left leg down and across the wicket so that he could turn the best of balls down to fine leg – a stroke that exasperated bowlers and could lead to unjustified but sometimes successful appeals for leg-before. This particular innings did not see Storer technically at his best, for he could have been out several times and he also scored at a more circumspect rate than usual; but granted the situation it was a performance of great resource.

For the last half hour before lunch he and his partner faced WG from the Pavilion end and Woods from the nursery, with Townsend coming off having bowled steadily rather than threateningly. Inevitably there was a loud cheer as WG took the ball and as usual he set his own field with much care. It included Mason and MacLaren in the deep and Woods immediately behind WG. The three-step run was a shuffle rather than a bustle and the arm was barely above the shoulder; but the first over to Storer produced an excited ' 's that' (with the 'how' lost in the beard), only for West to shake his head. At the other end Woods, who by this stage of his career claimed that he only pretended to bowl, was accurate enough without causing any special problems; and he gave the crowd some amusement by the nonchalent way in which he stopped a drive from Gunn with his foot. Progress up to lunch comprised mainly singles – some sharply taken – and Gunn in particular declined to hit even half-volleys. WG once or twice had Storer in two minds with his curling slows, had another appeal for leg-before turned down, and almost had him caught in the deep off a mishit, MacLaren just being unable to make enough ground from long on. In fact MacLaren by this time was emerging as the fielding star of the morning, with his work at third man to Woods featuring swooping pick-ups and lightning returns straight into MacGregor's gloves. Lord's after dry weather was a notoriously hard, unyielding turf to field on and MacLaren's virtuosity was particularly outstanding granted that he had been out of first-class cricket all summer. At lunch the score stood at 85 for two, with Gunn on 25, Storer on 29, and honours even after a tough opening session.

A leisurely interval lasted a whole hour, from two to three o'clock. On the ground there was something of a parade, in the Pavilion there was the usual unsatisfactory catering for members, and for the cricketers there was much to do apart from satisfying thirst and appetite. First after lunch came the customary ordeal by non-instamatic photography, with the backdrop for the teams on this occasion being the Assistant Secretary's garden behind the grandstand and Kortright distinguishing himself by being the only Gentleman without a blazer. There then took place something far more novel, which was a parade of the teams before the cinematograph. Moving film was only three years old and few of the cricketers would have been even aware of the invention's existence. Walking past in two curved lines, led by Shrewsbury and WG, they managed in the circumstances to combine dignity and naturalness surprisingly well, with the pipe-smoking Woods saying something funny to Lilley and Lockwood engaged in conversation with MacLaren. Stoddart and Brockwell (the latter especially dapper and jaunty) also smoked pipes and Kortright a cigarette. The fast bowler had by now hastily put on a jacket, turned up at the collar in a rather rebellious way; and he and Mason near the back of the parade broke rank by walking alongside each other, leaving Haigh and Alec Hearne to their own devices. The last cricketer, followed by umpires, officials and a bevy of solemn-looking hangers-on, was Rhodes. As was only right and proper, however, it was the man at the other end who stole the show, for just as he came past the camera and was about to go out of shot WG impishly raised his cap: it was the gesture of a man who would have been a media superstar in any age.

After lunch the weather became rather dull and oppressive, with clouds coming up heavily from the west and even a few spots of rain falling. The crowd by now was at its absolute maximum, with rows four or five deep sitting on the grass in front of the seats all the way round except in front of the Pavilion and somewhat encroaching on the field of play. The few police present kept a watchful eye and there was no disorder, though this did make the boundaries rather shorter. Indeed, the nearest to any crowd trouble that occurred during the day was when a man had to be removed from the grandstand after ignoring the sign 'No smoking allowed'. For everyone else there was the prospect of a long afternoon's cricket, which began with Kortright returning from the Pavilion end and being smacked through the off side by Gunn for four. Townsend at the other end kept the batsmen quiet, but as usual incident centred round the fast bowler: he nearly had Storer caught in the slips, but the batsman's riposte was a masterly leg-glide for four. Then, after only a quarter of an hour's play, WG was again seen leaving the field. Was the Old Man, the crowd wondered anxiously, suffering from the strain of it all?

Happily the reality was different, for WG was slipping away from the action in order to be Gloucestershire's official representative at an important meeting which had just begun in the Pavilion. MCC's President, the Hon. Alfred Lyttelton M.P., was in the chair and leading figures from all the first-class counties were present. They had come together in order to discuss Lord Hawke's contention that it was unfair that test matches in England should be played only at London and Manchester and his proposal that what was required was a new, formally constituted body, under the auspices of MCC, to be responsible for all aspects of home tests. His arguments were broadly accepted (with the silent concurrence of WG) and the upshot was the decision to create, not before time, what would become known as the Board of Control. It was yet another way in which the organisation of the game was becoming steadily more regularised.

Meanwhile, back in the arena, Haigh and then Rhodes were subbing for WG while their fellow professionals Gunn and Storer were beginning to cut loose. An uppish cut through the slips for four by Gunn off Townsend to bring up the hundred produced only subdued applause – because of the poor quality of the stroke – but he was soon loudly applauded for cutting and

on-driving Kortright to the boundary from successive deliveries. Kortright's response was in character: he dug the next ball in
short and hit Gunn hard on the left wrist, inducing a good deal
of rubbing. At the other end Storer cracked consecutive balls
from Townsend past point for four to reach his half-century,
shortly followed by Gunn as he took three twos and a single
from Kortright in a single over. He was still bowling at his
fastest, but with both batsmen thoroughly set neither he nor
Townsend could make an impression. Stoddart therefore made
a double change, bringing back Jackson from the nursery end
and at the other end drafting Mason into the attack. The Kent
captain's fast-medium stuff immediately checked the scoring,
and in his third over Storer lashed out a shade early and sent the
ball high to extra cover. Woods and Townsend converged, but
Stoddart's timely call of 'Sammy' prevented a collision and the
catch was taken easily enough. Storer had made 59 in just under
two hours and the score was 142 for three.

But if the Gentlemen had at last removed the troublesome
Derbyshire man, the bowling by now was coming all alike to
Billy Gunn. Over the years he and Shrewsbury had had the
reputation (and had often been criticised) for slow scoring and
excessive use of the pads, but on this showpiece occasion, having
overcome his early difficulties against Kortright and to a lesser
extent Townsend, he was giving a superb display, combining
to a remarkable degree the qualities of power and finish. His
stance may have been awkward (the two feet in a 'V' shape),
but his batting style as a whole was severely orthodox: with bat
half aloft in the manner of WG as the bowler approached, the
watchful face under a broad white sun hat prepared to make

full use of the natural blessings of an enormous reach allied to great suppleness of wrist and forearm strength. He stood still at the crease, only attempted to hit the bad ball, kept everything on the deck and studiously refrained from the pull. Most of the Gentlemen's bowling was on or outside the off stump and Gunn unfolded several of his very best off-drives. He also got the chance more than once to exhibit his own particular trademark, perhaps best described as a 'wide drive' between cover and point and invariably leaving the bat at great speed. It was not quite a cover drive, nor quite a slash, but something between the two; and placing his long left leg well down the wicket he would play it to stunning effect to any ball reasonably well pitched up on the off. Approaching the end of an illustrious career and clearly bent on a big score, he had rarely batted in more accomplished style than this afternoon.

His new partner at five to four was Tunnicliffe, warmly received as he came out to play his first major representative innings. Gunn greeted him by off-driving Jackson for four, and a minute or two later WG rejoined the game after his meeting. Mason then conceded four boundaries in quick succession, three to classy off-side strokes by Gunn and one to a lucky snick by Tunnicliffe, who was finding it hard to settle. All day the Gentlemen's fielding had never wanted for keenness, and a half-stop by WG at point prevented an otherwise certain four. At 166 WG brought himself back on for Mason and, though driven for four by Gunn and cut for three, managed in his second over to give the crowd the moment it had been waiting for: Tunnicliffe was persuaded to go for a chop behind point, got an edge and was well taken low down by MacGregor. There burst out a roar of applause, tempered only slightly by a feeling of disappointment that the tall Yorkshireman, out for 9, had failed to do himself justice.

Brockwell marched out to join Gunn and soon afterwards, from about half-past four, the light began to improve. He took longer than usual to get off the mark, but once he had hit Jackson square for four he proceeded to play a typically bright and bold innings against an attack that was starting to tire. Both batsmen punished WG and Jackson, and at one point there was a superb piece of cricket as Brockwell unleashed a magnificent off-drive against WG which Kortright at deep mid-off not only unexpectedly stopped with his left hand outstretched but returned so smartly that the batsmen failed to take a run. His colleagues joined in the crowd's approbation. WG tried Woods and Kortright again, but though Gunn went into his shell as he approached his century Brockwell batted as freely as before, his off-driving against Woods being especially crisp and well-timed. The total was 219 and the time a few minutes before five when Gunn, after batting for three hours, cut Kortright for four to reach his landmark. The whole house rose and WG led the fielding side's applause.

This was a trying phase for the Gentlemen, but in WG they had a leader who, though not the most subtle of captains, never allowed his own or his side's enthusiasm to flag. He now brought on Mason and Dixon, but Brockwell was especially severe on the latter, jumping out to his medium-pace deliveries in commanding fashion. Gunn for his part was evidently less than sated and continued to bat in an ominously even tenor. The nearest to a wicket was when Brockwell might have been run out by Townsend, who after fielding a hard stroke well at cover-point sent an inaccurate return. A brief respite, however, was at hand at ten past five, when the score was 240 for four. The tea interval was a new feature, imported from Australia and introduced this season. It had already aroused considerable criticism and a recent letter to the *Sportsman* had complained that in the match between Notts and Sussex it had extended to no less than twenty minutes. The regulations stated that the adjournment should only be taken if both captains agreed and that it was to last for not more than ten minutes; on this occasion it would have been a brave Arthur Shrewsbury who dissented from WG's wishes.

As the cricketers took their refreshment the crowd – officially numbered at 17,423, exclusive of members and guests – turned to scrutinise the various accounts in the evening papers of the earlier part of the day's play. Shouting by newspaper vendors was no longer allowed at Lord's, but the sporting ritual of reading about what one had just watched remained inviolable. The foreign news that afternoon was dominated by the war between the United States and Spain, with Santiago having just capitulated to American troops; nearer home the House of Commons was discussing the still remote possibility of introducing old-age pensions; and from Hoxton in the East End it was reported that the 4-lb loaf had fallen in price to 3¾d. None of these items was remotely as interesting as the report of the great match, but some no doubt checked the *Star* or the *Evening News* to make sure that George Robey was appearing that evening at the London Pavilion and Albert Chevalier at the Palace.

As play prepared to restart, the skies continued to clear and the sun shone pleasantly. Kortright was now tried at the nursery end, but by this stage he was a spent force, lacking pace and sting after being overbowled by WG. Brockwell twice drove him for four, while Dixon at the other end was equally ineffective. The runs mounted and WG turned to Jackson, ever reliable, and Townsend, whom he had been somewhat shielding during the afternoon. The move worked, for in the leg-spinner's second over Brockwell, having off-driven him along the ground for four, jumped out again and hit the ball hard and straight to Woods at mid-off. In just over an hour he and Gunn, with the brightest cricket of the day, had put on 94, of which his contribution was exactly half.

The score was now 272 for five. The neat Alec Hearne kept up the momentum with two pretty late-cuts to the boundary off Jackson, though he was missed at the wicket in MacGregor's only lapse of the day. WG again brought on Kortright at the Pavilion end, against all logic and to no avail, and just before six o'clock Gunn sent up the 300 with a delightful late-cut. At which point Woods belatedly replaced Kortright – at last sent out to graze for the rest of the day – and produced a spell worthy of his fighting reputation. He immediately bowled Hearne for 17 with a splendid ball and then at ten past six wholly deceived Gunn with a slow leg-stump yorker, which the batsman missed as he lunged forward far too early to try to play it to leg. Gunn had scored 139 in four hours, hit twenty-four boundaries and broken the individual Players' record in the fixture at Lord's. A grand, unstinting ovation accompanied him back to his dressing room. Following his dismissal the ensuing overs were rather anticlimactic, though wickets continued to fall. Lilley, playing in somewhat cramped style, was obdurate enough; but Townsend from the nursery end first deceived Lockwood (known for his weakness against leg spin) into playing back to a well-flighted, breaking ball that bowled him, and then trapped Haigh leg-before. The score was 328 for nine and the time just before half-past six.

There now took place the only major untoward episode of the day. As soon as Haigh was given out, the umpires pulled up the stumps and WG led his men off the field, even though the official card stated that stumps would be drawn at seven o'clock, as was usual at Lord's in June and July. Taken completely by surprise by this development were the ground men, who were not ready with their ropes and stakes; and before they had roped off the centre, hundreds of spectators were swarming over the wicket and inspecting it with much enthusiasm. It was, however, so bone hard that there was no question of damage being done. The likeliest explanation for this early cessation – no official reason was given – was that MCC were honouring WG that evening with a banquet in the Pavilion for which preparations needed to be made. This banquet was very much a private affair, and no reports of it would appear in the press.

Had the day as a whole fulfilled the cricketing world's almost inordinate expectations? The general consensus was that, despite the occasional *longueur*, the cricket had been fully worthy of the occasion; and that the enormous crowd had more than played its part through its enthusiastic but scrupulously impartial attention to the course of events. Moreover, with the weather apparently settled by the evening, the expectation was that the Gentlemen on the morrow would give a splendid display of batting and head the Players' total. And who knew, WG himself might even top it all with a century.

5

Tuesday

Between seven and eight o'clock in the morning a heavy fall of rain descended on north-west London, including the sacred, uncovered turf. The day's prospects were transformed, for a soft top would inevitably make batting a far more contingent affair than it had been the day before. But as the cricketers and their expectant public worked their way through their heavy cooked breakfasts, the big question remained: would the sun come out and render a difficult pitch an impossible one? By eleven o'clock, with play due to start in half an hour, the weather at Lord's was dull, oppressive and windless, the skies above leaden and threatening. Shrewsbury, who almost certainly had not been consulted by the MCC committee over team selection, must have wished already that his young Yorkshire reserve had been included in the eleven.

The uncertain outlook did not prevent another large crowd gathering; and the Stock Exchange correspondent of the *Financial Times* noted the absence of a good many members, lured to St John's Wood to see WG bat. By eleven o'clock there were some 7,000 people in the ground, and by twenty-five to twelve, when play began under continuing overcast conditions, the crowd was over 10,000. The batsmen were Lilley and J. T. Hearne, the bowlers Townsend and Woods, and after Lilley made a couple of good hits Hearne was completely deceived as he played forward to a slower one from Woods. The Players were all out for 335 after batting for just over five and a quarter hours.

Shrewsbury	c	Kortright	b Townsend	18
Abel			b Kortright	7
Gunn			b Woods	139
Storer	c	Woods	b Mason	59
Tunnicliffe	c	MacGregor	b Grace	9
Brockwell	c	Woods	b Townsend	47
Alec Hearne			b Woods	17
Lilley		not out		17
Lockwood			b Townsend	4
Haigh	lbw		b Townsend	9
J. T. Hearne			b Woods	1
		Bye 1, leg byes 7		8
			Total	335

Fall of Wickets:
1/25;2/29;3/142;4/178;5/272;6/302;7/311;8/316;9/328

	O	M	R	W
Kortright	37	13	90	1
Jackson	28	12	48	0
Townsend	25	8	58	4
Grace	12	2	34	1
Woods	20.1	4	49	3
Mason	11	3	30	1
Dixon	5	0	18	0

The Gentlemen required 216 to avoid being asked to follow on (the follow-on margin at that time being 120) and it seemed at best an even-money chance. But at least the wicket, having already been rolled for ten minutes before the start of play, would be rolled again between innings. Shortly before noon, at the end of another rather leisurely interval, the crowd was dispersed from the playing area with some difficulty and the Players took the field. It was noticed that Rhodes was subbing for Gunn, who had been hit badly on the knee by Kortright as well as severely on the wrist, though he was expected to bat again. Just as the clock struck twelve WG and Stoddart appeared at the Pavilion door and a hearty round of applause accompanied them to the wicket. The sun was still in, the light poor as WG took guard at the nursery end and as usual marked his exact spot with one of the bails. Though age meant that he now crouched slightly over his bat (relatively light at 2lb 5oz) he still made an imposing sight at the crease, with his great bulk, flowing beard and brawny forearms. His equipment was orthodox – he mistrusted skeleton pads and favoured gloves with big pieces of black indiarubber on the fingers – and in his stance all the weight was on his right leg, with his right foot firmly pivoted. By contrast his left foot was cocked up, some thought arrogantly. As the crowd hushed, unable to help itself from being fearful of the worst on such an occasion, WG adjusted his faded MCC cap, took a careful look round and, as he had so often in his life, prepared to face the bowling.

The man with the new ball was J. T. Hearne, operating from his beloved Pavilion end. He was a bowler who, despite a fairly long run, took little out of himself for his action was beautifully easy and rhythmic. He bowled off his toes, had his arm high and pointed his left shoulder almost towards short leg. He employed variations of line and flight and was never a mechanical bowler, but his abiding qualities were accuracy, length and a medium-fast break-back pitched on or just outside off stump. He could also bowl the one that went on with the arm. His field at this high noon of cricket's Golden Age was Tunnicliffe and Alec Hearne in the slips, Brockwell at third man, Shrewsbury at point, Haigh at cover-point, Lockwood at mid-off, Rhodes at long on, Abel at mid-on, Storer at forward short leg and Lilley standing up to the stumps. To the crowd's intense relief WG managed to survive the first ball and then the remaining four; but he was clearly very uncomfortable and twice was completely beaten. Cheer after cheer went up at the end of the over to mark its non-catastrophic conclusion, but WG and Stoddart hardly heard them as they busily patted the pitch.

On a rain-damaged wicket it was likely to be Lockwood who was the more fearsome proposition. His bowling action was a thing of menace as well as beauty: off a reasonably short run this man of no more than medium height would bound up to the wicket with springy, almost panther-like steps that flowed naturally into a graceful, upright delivery in which, not unlike a discus thrower, the right side of the body swung round in one piece and the right arm almost brushed against the ear. The ball he then delivered was usually fast-medium through the air and had an inward swerve accentuated by the way he used the full width of the crease; while off the pitch it would seem to gather pace as it broke back sharply and often got up. But Lockwood had no more dangerous delivery than his infamous slow one

('Not so very slow either,' WG once remarked) which few could spot and even fewer play. Over the years it had gained him many wickets, and in this his comeback season he was bowling it almost as well as ever. Stoddart took the over and, with Lilley standing well back, found the going almost as difficult as WG had, though he did get the third ball away to leg for a couple. With the ball rising unpleasantly he found himself defending body as much as wicket. Renowned as a bad-wicket batsman – indeed, rivalled only by Jackson among amateurs – Stoddart was facing one of his sterner challenges.

The next over saw WG off the mark with a single, but soon afterwards, facing Lockwood and without having added to his score, he gave the crowd palpitations. A short, climbing and very quick delivery made him take evasive action; the ball seemed to touch something; and with the other fielders shouting 'catch it', Lilley juggled with the ball and, after his third frantic snatch, spilled it. Was it a genuine, albeit theatrical, drop? Were he and the other Players under informal instructions to try to ensure that the Old Man made a decent score? If so, it is likely that they fell on Lockwood's deaf ears. Or did Lilley on his own initiative decide to take matters into (and out of) his own hands? We shall never know. But perhaps it is all academic, for while that drama was enacted some yards behind him WG all the time was pointedly rubbing his side. One run later and it was again almost curtains, as he spooned one back tamely to Hearne, who apparently was taken by surprise and failed to reach the ball. WG then changed his tactics and, deciding to attack Hearne, played some splendid forcing strokes, mostly to leg. A powerful on-drive sped to the ladies' seats, while in Hearne's next over a

magnificent pull cleared the ring of spectators, went right over
a carriage and pair and landed on the hotel terraces. This blow
earned him four runs, for the custom still remained in first-
class cricket that a ball had to be hit right out of the ground to
be a six; but for the crowd, by now getting over its trepida-
tion, it was a heart-warming moment. Hearne so far was below
his best, but Lockwood was fast, straight and kicking, giving
both batsmen a torrid time. Several of WG's strokes against
him were uppish, one just clearing Alec Hearne's head at slip,
and Stoddart concentratred solely on survival. It was a gripping
tussle and both batsmen did much gardening between overs.
Moreover, it was plain not only that the pitch was awkward but
also that WG's bruised heel had made him distinctly lame and
that he was moving with difficulty. He could have had a runner
if he had wished, but apparently he declined to countenance the
thought.

With the score on 28 after just over half an hour's play, WG
not out 22, Shrewsbury replaced Hearne with Haigh. The fast-
medium Yorkshireman – shortish, bowling in a cap and with
his dragging foot and rocking delivery taking far more out
of himself than either Hearne or Lockwood – opened with a
maiden. Stoddart then decided that enough was enough and,
in some desperation, pulled Lockwood to the boundary; and in
Haigh's next over a delightful leg glance for four was followed
next ball by an off-drive to the ropes. For someone who held
his bat so low down he could be remarkably powerful on the
front foot, driving with his arms rather than his body as a whole.
Off the next over WG twice edged Lockwood to the Pavilion
rails, both times just evading Alec Hearne, and thus brought up

the fifty in a highly creditable three-quarters of an hour. The
bowlers responded by turning the screw: Lockwood bowled
four successive maidens and Haigh, making the ball kick more
than Hearne had done, was almost as hard to get away, even
though WG had little difficulty turning his frequent attempted
yorkers into full tosses. At last, with the score on 56 after an
hour's batting, Stoddart in attempting to cut a rising ball from
Lockwood placed it straight to second slip, where Alec Hearne
completed the catch by hugging the ball to his chest just as he
seemed in danger of dropping it. Stoddart had scored 21 and,
though beaten many times by Lockwood, had done an important holding job.

So powerful was the Gentlemen's batting line-up that there
was much speculation about who would come in first wicket
down. Jackson it was, greeted by cheers, and the doughty struggle went on. Though the sun was conspicuous by its absence,
the wicket was still decidedly awkward and the batsmen continued often to have to stoop, as they had been doing all morning, in order to avoid flying deliveries. There was no end to
the gardening, and at one point WG caused intense amusement
to the crowd by stopping in the middle of a run to remove
something that had caught his eye. But it was painful as well as
assiduous work, and soon after Jackson had come in WG was
so sharply struck on his left hand by Haigh that he dropped the
bat like a red-hot cinder. Jackson too was in the wars, being
rapped on the thigh by Haigh. Almost as painful was the rate of
scoring, as the new man settled in and WG continued to play
back with much watchfulness. Eventually WG got Haigh away
through the slips for three, and almost immediately afterwards

the bowler thought he had Jackson caught behind: Haigh and Lilley appealed loudly; several fieldsmen joined in; umpire West was unbending; and Lilley appeared loth to part with the ball. The Yorkshireman then promptly cut Lockwood off successive balls for two and four, and with the batsmen starting to break free thoughts turned to the question of how much longer WG could go on without a runner, so lame was he becoming. The question was soon settled. WG had just cut Lockwood for four when, off a similarly rising ball to the one that claimed Stoddart, the Surrey bowler induced him to touch one to Lilley. This time he caught it cleanly – not even the most partisan follower of the Old Man could have expected a second slice of charity – and flung the ball gleefully to Tunnicliffe at slip. WG hobbled back to an ovation, having made 43 in an hour and a half. It had not been one of his commanding innings, and at no stage had he seemed wholly settled, but all agreed that in the context of the wicket, the bowling and the occasion it had been a thoroughly worthy display.

Inevitably the bloom of the day was felt to be gone, as to general surprise Townsend came in ahead of either MacLaren or Mason. WG's protégé never looked like staying and, after glancing Lockwood gracefully for a couple, he played too soon at the same bowler's slower one and sent a gentle return catch. Perhaps he had been overawed, or perhaps he had been put off by the two short legs posted for him; in any event the regret felt at his failure was widespread. MacLaren followed in and, on making his first batting appearance of the season, was so heartily cheered that he felt compelled to acknowledge the reception. This favourite of the crowd was quickly off the mark, but then faced Hearne, who was back at the Pavilion end after Jackson had driven Haigh for four. Hearne bowled him the most testing of maidens, each of the five balls finely-pitched, but MacLaren survived. At the other end Lockwood, encouraged by the drying wicket, his three successes and the fact that the sun at last had come out, was still full of fire even though he had been bowling for over an hour and a half. Three times in the space of ten minutes he hit MacLaren on the fingers as the batsman stretched forward to balls that rose up from a good length – as many times as MacLaren expected to be hit on the hand in the course of a whole season. Lockwood also completely beat him with a ball that whipped across the leg side and went for four byes. But the two old Harrovians grimly stuck it out and, exercising the utmost caution, took the score up to 99 for three at lunch, which as usual was at two o'clock. Jackson was on 23, MacLaren on 3, and overall the Gentlemen had fared better during the morning's play than had seemed likely at the outset.

Around the ring, talk over the pork pies and bottled beer was much of WG but also of 'Jacker', who had shown all his well-known skill and resilience in adverse conditions. He was a batsman who never altered his methods according to the state of the wicket, though undoubtedly he had given so far a less free display than usual, if equally finished. One of his great defensive strengths was the way in which he used the 'half-cock' stroke, modelled on WG, to keep the ball down; while anything overpitched he was always quick to drive. But as ever what had shone through on this occasion had been Jackson's flawless temperament: the thought of failure never crossed his mind; and as he re-fastened the straps of his pads he would have looked forward to the afternoon with equanimity. Meanwhile, the crowd outside had grown almost as dense as on the first day, being officially 14,633 paid plus members and friends, in all not far short of 20,000. With the sun having gone back in after its brief appearance, to be replaced again by heavy clouds, there was reason to think that the wicket would gradually ease during the afternoon, provided that the rain held off. The atmosphere remained rather oppressive and still, fitting conditions for an intense contest intently watched.

Hearne continued from the Pavilion end and at once inadvertently brought up the hundred with four byes, a fine ball defeating both Jackson and Lilley (standing up). At the other end it was still Lockwood, who was starting to be overbowled by Shrewbury even more than Kortright had been by WG. In his first over MacLaren jumped out to him in Jessopian fashion, but before the ball had been delivered, completely missed the slower one that ensued and should have been stumped by Lilley standing back. The wicket-keeper however threw wildly and a bye was run. MacLaren in the wake of this episode reverted for the most part to his rather cramped pre-luncheon style, but Jackson began to take advantage of the palpable improvement in the pitch and also Lockwood's overlong exertions. In one over he took eleven off him, mostly well-played cuts but including a flukey snick to leg. That brought him only two away from his half-century, but off the first ball of the next over, bowled by Hearne, he was neatly caught behind by Lilley, now standing back. He had been batting for just under an hour and a half and the score was 137 for four.

At this point, with Mason walking out at ten past three in place of Jackson, Archie MacLaren may well have reflected that for a class batsman he had so far failed to do himself justice and that, with the wicket now becoming more amenable, it was time to show that he could play strokes and not just occupy the crease. Even at this stage in his career he had the reputation for being a batsman in the grand manner. He stood up to his full height with bat raised well behind him poised for an uninhibited swing; he rarely compromised in his movements, going either all the way forward or all the way back; and of course, as later immortalised by Beldam's photography, he loved to jump out to drive with a glorious, unstinting swing of the shoulders. He also had a marvellous hook (played with forearm, not wrist) and pull, as well as a particular skill at forcing good-length balls to the on side. MacLaren was not a tall man, but he was muscularly powerful and very quick on his feet; and altogether he was the most thrusting and decisive of batsmen. Yet he was also a fighting batsman and someone who, it is easy to forget, had had to work hard at his game, mentally as much as anything, in order to flourish at the highest level. Playing in this particular match meant a great deal to him and he was determined not to let himself or WG down.

He was further inspired by his new partner, Mason, who started with two driven boundaries off Hearne. Then MacLaren began: first a big on-drive off Lockwood finished in the ladies' enclosure, where a lady in a pink dress renewed the applause for the hit by capably throwing the ball back; and then in one memorable over, which included two no-balls for overstepping, he took the Surrey man apart with a series of thrilling strokes, notably a lofty straight drive, an on-drive, a cut and an off-drive. The yield for the over was sixteen, all but one scored by MacLaren, and at last Lockwood took his sweater. At the other end Alec Hearne with his mixed spin had already replaced his cousin and, although unlucky to be snicked by Mason for a rapidly-run five, he and Haigh managed for a few overs to slow the scoring. But then MacLaren came again and played two marvellous off-drives against Hearne – the second of them, which cleared the Pavilion rails and landed in front of the Players' dressing room, bringing up his half-century amidst scenes of unreserved enthusiasm. Sadly it was too good to last; and the next ball he received from Haigh he skied to cover-point, where Abel had plenty of time to think about Kortright, the universe and everything before taking a well-judged catch. The cheers rang out for MacLaren as he returned to the Pavilion, for he and Mason had put on sixty in only thirty-five minutes and, by taking the Gentlemen to within twenty of the target to avoid the follow-on, had transformed the match in the most spectacular manner possible.

The new batsman was Dixon and it was clear from the outset that, as a good Nottinghamshire man, his policy would be to keep one end going while his partners enjoyed themselves. Mason continued to bat attractively, in his polished and correct way, and by four o'clock (with the light starting to deteriorate) the follow-on was saved. Soon afterwards J. T. Hearne returned to the Pavilion end to replace his ineffective cousin and, after being late-cut for four, had Mason brilliantly caught for 35 by Tunnicliffe at slip, high up with his left hand. It was almost his only false stroke in a good innings, though for the most part played on an improving wicket against the lesser bowlers. The popular Woods got his usual hearty reception and played his usual hearty game: thirteen runs off eight balls, including a high-driven four into the Pavilion, before Hearne bowled him all over the shop. He was followed by Wynyard, batting surprisingly low down the order but, despite a vigorous hit to the square-leg scoreboard, he was never at home; and after Dixon had been missed by Tunnicliffe from a difficult chance off Haigh's bowling, the Hampshire captain skied Hearne to third man and was easily caught by Brockwell. The time was twenty-five to five, the score 252 for eight, and Dixon had calmly gathered a dozen runs in a little over three-quarters of an hour.

MacGregor began cautiously in poor light but soon played a couple of pleasing off-drives, prompting Shrewsbury to bring on the medium-fast Brockwell at the nursery end in place of the somewhat disappointing Haigh. It was Hearne, however, who dislodged him, getting him caught behind by his opposite number. The last man was Kortright, who to the crowd's delight proceeded to bat with far more skill, including a nice cut off Brockwell, than he was generally credited with. Moreover, realising it was now or never, Dixon began to open out, despatching loose balls to the off-side boundary with precision. A slashing off-drive by Kortright off Brockwell rattled to the boundary, earning the biggest cheer of the day. Shrewsbury responded with a double change – Alec for J.T. and Lockwood for Brockwell – and with his fourth ball Lockwood secured a richly-deserved fourth wicket when he had Dixon well caught low down by Storer in the slips. The batsman was not satisfied and stood his ground, but Phillips raised his finger. The Gentlemen were all out for 303 at twenty-five past five, having batted for four hours and forty minutes; and Dixon's patient, valuable 31 had taken just under a hundred minutes.

W. G. Grace	c	Lilley	b	Lockwood	43
A. E. Stoddart	c	A. Hearne	b	Lockwood	21
F. S. Jackson	c	Lilley	b	J. T. Hearne	48
C. L. Townsend	c	and	b	Lockwood	2
A. C. MacLaren	c	Abel	b	Haigh	50
J. R. Mason	c	Tunnicliffe	b	J. T. Hearne	35
J. A. Dixon	c	Storer	b	Lockwood	31
S. M. J. Woods			b	J. T. Hearne	13
Captain E. G.					
Wynyard	c	Brockwell	b	J. T. Hearne	12
G. MacGregor	c Lilley		b	J. T. Hearne	16
C. J. Kortright		not out			17
		Byes 11, leg byes 4			15
				Total	303

Fall of Wickets:
1/56; 2/79; 3/85; 4/137; 5/197; 6/222; 7/236; 8/252; 9/273

	O	M	R	W
J. T. Hearne	33	10	87	5
Lockwood	32.4	9	82	4
Haigh	31	12	64	1
A. Hearne	11	2	36	0
Brockwell	6	1	19	0

The Players were left with fifty minutes' batting in light thought by many to be bad enough to warrant an appeal. WG did not take the field and clemency was shown to Rhodes, who had been fielding almost the whole day for Gunn and had done a lot of excellent work on the Pavilion boundary. Instead the substitute was 'Bob' Carpenter, the Essex batsman and a member of the ground staff at Lord's. His father, playing for Cambridgeshire, had been perhaps the greatest professional batsman of the mid-Victorian era. Stoddart as deputy captain was disinclined to be chivalrous and led off with his two fastest bowlers, Kortright and Woods. The demon was again at his very fastest, keen to redress his ill luck of the previous day, and must have been extremely difficult to pick out against the Pavilion, then as for many years afterwards without a sight-screen: so much so that someone in the press box wondered aloud whether Kortright would be accused of murder or manslaughter if he killed one of the professionals. Neither Shrewsbury nor Abel could time the ball and Abel in particular was anxiety personified. Ten minutes was enough: in the same over that he square-cut Kortright for four, he was comprehensively bowled by a low full-toss that pitched on the base of his leg stump and sent it flying several yards. The crowd roared and Abel somewhat ignominiously retired. The Hon. R. H. Lyttelton in the Pavilion thought it the most painful of sights to see a batsman so palpably running away from a bowler; but the 'Guv'nor' had the last word, for when accused soon afterwards of having displayed cowardice he replied with unanswerable logic, 'Well, I am the father of six children, and there are plenty of other bowlers to make runs off besides Mr Kortright.'

With Gunn not sorry to be *hors de combat* until the morrow, Storer filled the breach and, despite having his bat knocked out of his hands thrice in ten minutes by Kortright, showed himself as pugnacious as ever. Both bowlers were finding the edge and applause again and again greeted MacLaren's remarkably fine fielding at short third man. It was a situation that Shrewsbury found little to his taste, even though the light was marginally improving, and after cutting Woods for four he had the top of his off stump clipped by the same bowler as he tried to hit out. He and Abel had managed between them a match aggregate of forty-one runs. At 21 for two, with almost half an hour left, it was a critical time for the Players, and for twenty minutes the new man Tunnicliffe did little more than keep the bowlers out. But at the other end Storer, batting with complete confidence, took the attack to them and twice hit Kortright to leg for four, once off a ball that rose nearly as high as his head. It was a fine exhibition of coolness and courage. Near the end Townsend was given a turn at the nursery end in place of Woods, but was unable to prevent the batsmen reaching the safe harbour of half-past six. The Players' score stood at 42, with Storer on 21 and Tunnicliffe on 5.

There were many talking points at the end of an eventful day's play but general agreement that the Gentlemen had done marvellously well to overcome their meteorological misfortune and that the two outstanding performers of the day had been Jackson and Lockwood. Much satisfaction was taken in the innings of WG and MacLaren, as well as in the epic quality of the batsmen's struggle in the morning against high-class bowling and keen fielding. Everyone accepted that Shrewsbury had been unlucky not to have Rhodes at his disposal, but some wondered whether even so he had made the best possible use of his resources: in particular it was felt that he should have taken off Lockwood much sooner and thus been able to bring him back earlier, and also that he should have tried Storer with his leg-breaks.

What of prospects for the final day? The majority opinion among the cricket correspondents was that the match would be drawn and the *Daily Chronicle* even expressed regret that a further day had not been set aside in order to ensure a result. No one backed the Players to win, but only the *St James's Gazette* went out on a limb and declared that it would not be greatly surprised to see the Gentlemen gain a brilliant victory. All expected another interesting day's play, with at least the possibility of a good finish.

But before then there was business to be done on the Tuesday evening. The Cricketers' Fund Friendly Society was holding its annual meeting and among those who attended in the members' dining room at Lord's were J. T. Hearne, Storer and West the umpire. Also present was Lord Harris, a strong supporter of the Fund, which had been in existence since 1857 for the purpose of mitigating the effects of old age, illness and accident on professional cricketers and their dependants. It also sought to make sure that all members had a decent burial. The Fund over the years had done much good work, though it was made clear at this meeting that expenses due to death and sickness had recently been outrunning income. Harris, never backward in coming forward, favoured a general appeal, because he felt that the public would be willing to help deserving men disabled in the course of their professional employment; and he would look to the MCC committee to support the movement. None of the professionals expressed a view. The election of new members (including Rhodes) finished the formal proceedings and there then followed that most hallowed of Victorian rituals on such occasions, a smoking concert.

Meanwhile, a few miles away, a rather different function was taking place at the Sports Club in St James's Square. This was a dinner for WG, presided over by Sir Richard Webster, the Attorney-General. It was attended by the entire Gentlemen's team, the presidents of county cricket clubs, many well-known cricketers and members of the club, the company numbering in all upwards of 150. After some preliminary speeches and toasts Webster, who was also Surrey's president, submitted the main toast of the evening – 'WG' – and served up some well-known jokes ('What are the three Christian graces?' 'Grace before meat, grace after meat, and W. G. Grace') and stories (including WG's hurdling achievements as a young man). He concluded by declaring to cheers that they all owed a great debt to WG because he had elevated the national game, never thinking of himself but always of cricket. After the toast itself had been greeted with musical honours, WG rose to his feet amidst prolonged cheers. He was not someone who enjoyed public speaking ('I would any day as soon make a duck as a speech,' he once remarked), but now there was no alternative. The highly characteristic speech that followed brings us as near as we can ever come *in extenso* to the authentic voice of the man himself:

I cannot find words in which to express my feelings for the very kind way in which Sir Richard Webster has spoken of me tonight. I have not deserved half of it. ('*Yes*') But no matter about that. I can only say you have tonight done me the greatest honour you have ever done me. When I look round, and see the friends and cricketers near me – (*hear, hear*) – I wish I had Stoddart's happy knack of saying the right words in the right place. If I cannot say the right words, I feel them. (*cheers*) You all know my speeches are few and short. When I am pleased they may be all right. When I am not they may be all wrong. (*great laughter*) I hope tonight it will be all right. (*hear, hear*) There is only one drawback, and that is that Sir Richard Webster has said so many things that I do not deserve at all. ('*No*') As to a hurdle race being a hard race, it may be so when you have anyone to run against you, but on the occasion you have mentioned four or five started, and only one finished. (*laughter*) I was that lucky one. (*cheers*) To get back to cricket. Sir Richard Webster said I was always very good to young players. (*hear, hear*) Well, I remember, many years ago, when I was playing for MCC against Surrey, at Lord's, they brought up an unfortunate colt, who had taken a few wickets in a match the week before. He bowled one over. The first ball I played back quietly to him. The next went into the garden, down by the old armoury; the third followed suit, and the fourth and fifth went into the Pavilion. They never bowled that poor fellow again. (*laughter*) If you call that giving advice to a young cricketer, well – (*great laughter*) Sir Richard Webster says I have been very lucky bowling lately. The other day I was down at Leyton, and my friend Kortright was there. Very shortly afterwards I got a telegram saying: 'Why did you bowl out the poor old colts?' (*laughter*) Down at Bristol Sammy Woods said: 'When you see the colts coming you say "Give me the ball," and out they go.' (*laughter*) Sammy calls them rabbits. (*laughter*) I should like to have seen some of these rabbits in today, when we were batting, and Kortright bowling on the same wicket. (*Hear, hear and laughter*) I am very proud to be captain of the lot we have got here tonight. I have played on a good many wickets, and I know when they are a little bad, and I can tell you to get over 300 runs on the wicket we have played on today was better than we expected. (*cheers*) My old friend Stoddart and myself, when we got 50, thought we had done pretty well. (*hear, hear*) The 300 wasn't made by one man, but by everybody on the side. (*hear, hear*) I must say if we had won the toss the game would have been nearly over tonight. (*hear, hear*) I can only say I thank you very much for the very kind way in which the toast has been proposed and received. (*cheers*)

Toasts to 'Cricket' and the chairman having been drunk, the proceedings concluded and eleven Gentlemen repaired to their respective homes, hotels and clubs somewhat the worse for wear.

6

Wednesday

NO RAIN FELL overnight and at eleven o'clock the forecast for the rest of the day was 'fair, warmer'; but as play was about to start just after half-past, such a chill wind was blowing from the east that overcoats and even ulsters would not have been out of place. The dull, threatening weather affected the attendance, as did the fact of it being the third day, and although the crowd was perfectly respectable there were plenty of empty seats to be had during the morning's play. Carpenter continued to act as substitute for WG, nursing an injured hand (following his blow from Haigh) as well as his bruised heel, so it was Stoddart who led out the Gentlemen.

He began as he had ended the previous evening, with Kortright and Townsend offering a marked contrast in pace. It was apparent from the early exchanges that the wicket had lost its last vestiges of rain-affected devil; and though Kortright bowled at his fastest and gave Storer a couple of nasty knocks, one on the knuckles and another on the hip, neither batsman was in serious trouble. Tunnicliffe was the longer to play himself in, but soon both were setting out their stalls, with Carpenter at mid-off distinguishing himself by stopping some hard drives. They also stole several short singles and on one occasion brought the

crowd to life when Tunnicliffe blocked a ball from Kortright:
Storer called for the run and then raced Kortright down the
pitch, culminating in the doubtless exasperated bowler kicking
the ball at the stumps and just missing them, with Storer still a
yard or two short. In due course Jackson and Woods took up the
bowling, the latter bowling fast and erratically from the Pavilion
end. One of his balls, a beamer, was totally unsighted by Storer,
who only avoided being felled by diving to the ground at the
last moment. But the scoring mounted – one over from Jackson
cost eleven – and so did the impudence of the running, matched
by the keenness of the fielding. One direct hit at the bowler's
end from MacLaren at mid-off failed to run out Tunnicliffe, but
rebounded from the stumps and caught Woods a painful blow
on the shin. He, however, made light of it and at once went on
with his over, being cut cleverly and late to the boundary by
Storer to bring up the hundred after just under an hour's play.

Trying to decide how to break this flourishing partnership
was Jackson, who a few minutes earlier had assumed authority
after Stoddart for an unspecified reason had left the field. Rhodes
came out as the second substitute. Soon after Storer completed
his second half-century of the match, the new captain turned to
Mason's fast-medium, bowled with a high arm, easy action and
moving away a little. His first over from the Pavilion end proved
disastrous, as Storer plundered it for ten, including a searing hit
over point's head; but Mason then went round the wicket and
was driven by Tunnicliffe straight into the hands of Rhodes
at extra-cover. The stand had realised 106 at a critical stage of
the match and Tunnicliffe's patient 44, redeeming his first-
innings failure, earned him a good hand as he returned to the

Players' room. The new batsman, somewhat bruised and lame, was Gunn, who despite his handicaps now batted even more fluently than he had done on Monday. A scorching square-cut off Kortright got him off the mark and showed who was master. At the other end Storer twice cut Mason for four, the second hit going off Jackson's forearm at some considerable speed to the boundary. But Jackson then brought Townsend on at the nursery end in place of Kortright, and almost at once Storer, three short of his thousand runs for the season, succumbed to the temptation of a well pitched up, spinning ball and was very competently caught by Rhodes at mid-off. Did nine Gentlemen converge on the young pro to slap him on the back after this second catch in quick time? History does not relate. In any case, Storer was out for a meritorious, practically faultless 73; and with the Players' score standing at 147 for four the match was again nicely poised.

Even more so when Brockwell was soon smartly caught and bowled by Woods off a hard, head-high drive; and a few minutes later Gunn was perhaps lucky to survive a strong lbw appeal from Townsend, fully shared by MacGregor behind the stumps. But from that point the Players regained the initiative, with Gunn batting superbly (eight boundaries in his first 34 and twice in an over lifting Woods to the Pavilion rails) and Alec Hearne steadily supporting him. Together they added 41 in half an hour before Mason, brought back into the attack by the returned Stoddart, was able to use his height to extract enough life from the pitch to get Hearne caught behind. The reliable Lilley joined Gunn and they were together at two o'clock, Gunn not out 44, Lilley not out 4, and the score 203 for six.

By this time the ground had filled up nicely, with almost 10,000 paying spectators and some two to three thousand members and friends filling the Pavilion and special enclosures. The weather had also brightened somewhat, though the sun came out only intermittently; and there was every prospect of a full afternoon's cricket. With the Players 235 runs on and four wickets in hand, might Shrewsbury contemplate a declaration fairly soon after lunch? Few can have deemed it probable: for he was not only a naturally cautious man, but also he would have been very conscious of the almost unprecedented batting strength of the Gentlemen, a phenomenon much vaunted by the sporting press during the previous few days and to a large degree borne out by their depth of performance in the first innings, with only Townsend failing to reach double figures. The very last thing Shrewsbury would do would be to hand this particular match on a plate to WG.

On resumption an off-drive and cut off Kortright took Gunn to his half-century, but soon afterwards he was caught behind off Mason for 56, made in eighty-five minutes and including only five singles. It had been an altogether brilliant innings, confirming him as without question the batsman of the match. Lockwood came in and looked uncomfortable against Kortright, bowling with renewed speed despite another excessive workload; and he skied one towards long leg, where Wynyard made a gallant but unavailing attempt to catch it on the run. But at the other end Mason dismissed Lilley, who cut the ball hard and low only to be magnificently caught left-handed by the diving Stoddart. The crowd, probably the most critical and sophisticated of the three days, rose and cheered as one man. Then off the first ball of the next over Lockwood's middle stump was sent flying by a Kortright special. At 237 for nine and the time twenty past three the match again seemed open, certainly if Kortright could do the business. But J. T. Hearne and Haigh met him and Mason with broad bats, added twenty-six useful runs, and in the event it needed the return of Woods to take the last wicket, having Hearne caught by Stoddart at mid-off. The innings closed at a quarter to four, having lasted for four and a quarter hours.

Shrewsbury			b	Woods	11
Abel			b	Kortright	5
Storer	c	sub	b	Townsend	73
Tunnicliffe	c	sub	b	Mason	44
Gunn	c	MacGregor	b	Mason	56
Brockwell	c	and	b	Woods	5
A. Hearne	c	MacGregor	b	Mason	11
Lilley	c	Stoddart	b	Mason	10
Lockwood			b	Kortright	6
Haigh		not out			12
J. T. Hearne	c	Stoddart	b	Woods	13
		Byes 9, leg byes 8			17
					263

Fall of Wickets:
1/11; 2/21; 3/127; 4/147; 5/152; 6/193; 7/226; 8/237; 9/237

	O	M	R	W
Kortright	36	8	83	2
Woods	26	9	62	3
Townsend	15	4	33	1
Jackson	9	4	21	0
Mason	17	8	47	4

The general expectation between innings was that a draw was now inevitable: with the official card stating that stumps would be drawn at half-past six, this gave the Gentlemen only two and a half hours to score 296, hardly a realistic possibility against Lockwood and J. T. Hearne; while it was equally implausible that the Players in that time could bowl out such a strong batting side, especially as the wicket so far had been showing few signs of third-day wear and tear. As the cricketers came out just after four o'clock there was a sigh of disappointment when it was seen that the injured WG was holding himself back, but some compensation in the sight of MacLaren as Stoddart's opening partner.

Lockwood began from the nursery end. His first ball was steered by MacLaren for a single; his third, well pitched up, was hit by Stoddart in front of point for four; and his last of the over, a rising ball, had Stoddart nicely caught by Tunnicliffe low down at slip. The battle was on, and over the next half hour MacLaren and Jackson had their work cut out against Lockwood and J. T. Hearne, both bowling extremely well. Jackson was the freer and four times got Hearne away to the ropes, mainly to the off side. But they each needed some good fortune, Jackson when he edged Hearne just wide of cousin Alec at second slip and MacLaren when he might have been given leg-before to Lockwood. The score had gone up to 41 when MacLaren was out rather unluckily. Playing back to Hearne he hit the ball hard on to one of his pads, whence it rolled back and knocked off the bails. Seemingly powerless to stop the course of events MacLaren was clearly much vexed as he left the crease, and the crowd shared his disappointment.

There then followed a sensational ten minutes. It was apparent that WG still had hopes of a famous victory, for he now sent in his hitters. First came the redoubtable Woods. He was his customary aggressive self and scored nine runs off the first four balls he faced, nearly being caught by Gunn off a lofted drive; but the next ball from Hearne bowled him, as he played on to his off stump. 55 for three and enter Wynyard. He had the reputation of being a shaky starter and indeed failed to last the over, being bowled as he tried to glance to leg. 55 for four and the first duck of the match. It was now Lockwood's turn. Jackson took a single, but off the last ball of the over Mason was clean bowled by a very fast ball that seemed to keep low. 56 for five and the second duck of the match. Townsend now came in, only to see Jackson bowled for 33 by Hearne off the first ball of the next over. 56 for six, the crowd in a state of high excitement, and the umpires working overtime to put back the stumps.

Clearly it was not distinguished batting, and it is probable that the Gentlemen, with their propensity for the drive, were tending to commit themselves too early to the front foot and getting bowled through the gate. Nevertheless, in defence of the batsmen, subsequent enquiry revealed that Hearne, bowling rather slower than usual, had found some broken spots on the wicket and, getting prodigious work on the ball, was making it break down the Lord's slope as much as eight or nine inches. It also transpired that the balls which bowled Wynyard and Jackson had brushed their pads, though in both cases they were fairly beaten. But whatever the cause it was a collapse that left the Gentlemen, at just gone five o'clock, in a pretty pickle – especially as it was freely rumoured around the ground that WG (who had been seen between innings communicating something to the press box in the grandstand) had such a badly bruised hand that he would be unable to bat.

It was a situation tailor-made for the stolid Dixon, though less so for the inexperienced, naturally attacking Townsend. But both batsmen buckled down against keen bowling and close-set fields and, over the next quarter of an hour, only three singles were scored, all by Townsend. His first brought quite a cheer as he drove Hearne; and that the sympathies of the crowd were with the hard-pressed batsmen was shown by the cries of 'bravo' at the end of each over, even a maiden. Soon after Townsend had leg glanced Hearne for four, Shrewsbury brought on Haigh for Lockwood; and off his first ball Dixon after twenty-five minutes at the crease at last got off the mark, ironical cheers greeting his short single from an on-side push. Townsend began to open up, twice hitting Hearne to leg for four; but his new-found freedom did not last, for with the score on 77 he edged Hearne low and fast to slip, where Tunnicliffe rolled over as he took another excellent catch. The time was twenty-five to six and the Gentlemen once again were staring down the prover-bial barrel.

But cometh the hour, cometh the doctor. After a tantalising pause of a minute or more a mighty shout followed by tremen-dous cheering signified his appearance hobbling down the Pavilion steps. It was several minutes before he faced the bowl-ing, but he then played out a maiden to Hearne. At the other end Dixon managed to keep out one yorker from Haigh, but the second, somewhat slower, went through his defences and bowled him. 77 for eight. Now joined by MacGregor, WG got off the mark with a block to the on side. The Middlesex keeper, however, was not long in the middle, for with the score at 80 a slower ball from Hearne gave him his quietus. Nine wickets down, three-quarters of an hour left, and hardly anyone on the ground gave the Gentlemen a chance of avoiding a humiliating defeat. Quite a few spectators left to catch early trains, while those in the popular parts were gathering themselves and their belongings together in anticipation of the final rush over the field.

A bareheaded, determined-looking Kortright strode in briskly to join his old sparring partner. Were they by now on speaking terms? Perhaps, for Kortright, many years later, would remember their crisp exchange as he reached the middle. 'Korty, don't be nervous, play your usual game.' 'All right, Doc, I'll do my best.' Kortright over the years had played some good innings for Essex and on his day was a handsome striker of the ball, but suffered from the besetting fault of impetuosity. His first ball from Hearne was almost his last, but he survived the rest of the over and even got off the mark. Haigh's five balls did not threaten, so it was back to Hearne. His first two were stinging deliveries to which WG had to get right back on his stumps to keep out. The third was more pitched up and WG went for a big hit, but failed to get hold of the ball properly. It went over mid-on, where Abel turned, threw off his cap and went for the catch for all he was worth, but was a yard short when the ball pitched. The crowd breathed again. Over the next few overs the last pair settled down to make a stand of it: Kortright, after a lucky snick or two, played some powerful strokes, especially straight drives,

while WG with his swollen hand was more defensive, playing
Hearne far more comfortably than any of the earlier batsmen. As
hopes began to rise that the Gentlemen might yet avert defeat
the excitement around the ground became ever more manifest. The clock was anxiously gazed at, the end of every over
acclaimed and even the smallest incident cheered. 'Well done,
Grace!' was shouted again and again when WG late-cut a fast
one from Lockwood (who had returned to the attack) through
the slips to the boundary; and soon afterwards a great round of
applause greeted Kortright's off-drive to the Pavilion rails off
Hearne that brought up the hundred.

Twenty minutes to go. Kortright was batting with much
confidence and at last enjoying some of the luck that had so
deserted him when he had been bowling. The occasional ball
from Hearne was too good for him, but fortuitous edges saved
him. At the other end WG calmly took most of Lockwood.
With the score on 114, Shrewsbury turned to spin and brought
on Alec Hearne in place of his cousin, but though he bowled
some testing deliveries the batsmen refused to let their concentration waver. Out in the ring the suspense mounted and the
clock on the outside of the tennis court seemed to be going
backwards. Somehow it crawled round to twenty-seven minutes
past six and Shrewsbury decided to replace Lockwood at the
nursery end with Storer. The Derbyshire man bowled occasional leg spin – sometimes penetratingly, often erratically – and
with Kortright facing the Players' captain no doubt hoped to
tempt him to take a risk. 'Time!' came the cries from all parts of
the ground as Storer bowled a few trial balls along the side of the
pitch, but umpire West did not agree and the over proceeded. A

cheer went up after each ball, but the crowd need hardly have worried for the over turned out to be an assortment of slow long hops that Kortright calmly despatched for a total of six runs. The match was saved.

Kortright breathed a sigh of relief and turned towards the Pavilion, the spectators rent the air with a great shout, and the massed hordes at the ropes began their rush. To their surprise they found the fieldsmen earnestly waving them back and telling them that play would go on until seven. This not unnaturally led to some murmurs of discontent, for it was felt that WG and Kortright had already fairly saved the game and deserved to carry their bats out. However, the prospect of another half hour of such an exciting contest was enough to soothe the malcontents, and before long everyone was back behind the ropes. Altogether it was a moment of some bathos, for what no one had troubled to tell the crowd at large was that earlier in the day the two captains had agreed to an extra half hour in the event of a result seeming likely. More than one observer commented that it would have been quite easy for the authorities to have sent a dozen people round the ground before the Gentlemen's innings began in order to put the crowd in the picture about this arrangement. Nor was it only the crowd that was kept in the dark, for Kortright himself (as he later avowed) had always thought half-past six was his target. Presumably he and his captain had not gone in for much chatting between overs.

The score stood at 130 as extra time began. Over the next quarter of an hour Shrewsbury tried a series of bowling changes, bringing on Haigh, Brockwell and J. T. Hearne in rapid succession. WG drove Haigh to the Pavilion for four and

Kortright hit several boundaries, all wildly cheered. At a quarter to seven WG hobbled down the pitch and shook hands with Kortright, a public ending of the well-bruited antagonism between them that evoked a demonstration of approval. It also nearly presaged the end, for soon after Kortright was all but bowled by Hearne and WG himself almost succumbed to a yorker. Meanwhile, with the overs being bowled at quickfire speed, the tension around the ground had become well-nigh unbearable: every ball was punctuated with a frantic round of applause; old hands in the press box could hardly restrain themselves from rising in their seats and cheering with the multitude; and if umbrella handles were not being steadily gnawed away they should have been. An increasingly desperate Shrewsbury even tried two overs of Abel, but his innocuous slows failed to do the trick. The time on the clock was four minutes to seven when the veteran captain, acknowledged as a master tactician supreme in his understanding of the game, played his last card.

Just as the sun suddenly came out from the clouds behind the Pavilion he brought on Lockwood at that end for the first time in the match. The great bowler pulled off his sweater with a meaningful jerk. Kortright, not out 46 and with the sun full in his face, stopped the first ball. And the second. 'Well played, well played,' came the squeaky voice from the other end. But the third ball paid for all, for it was the feared slower one, bowled by Lockwood without any perceptible change of action. Kortright played a lunging drive outside his off stump, failed to get to the pitch, and the ball spun away high over cover-point, where Haigh running backwards and to his right brought off a finely-judged catch. The Players had won by 137 runs and the Old Man was left high and dry on 31 not out.

The crowd gave a gasp and a groan and then, with the match indubitably over, rushed on to the field of play and surged round WG as he limped back to the Pavilion. One of the first to congratulate the two batsmen on their stand of 78 was Jack Hearne, while WG himself generously slipped an arm into Kortright's in appreciation of his sterling if ultimately unavailing efforts. At last the cricketers left the arena and the spectators crowded round the Pavilion, cheering and shouting themselves hoarse with appreciative plaudits. They called upon the heroes of the fight to make their acknowledgements and, after a while, the champion was seen to be leading Kortright by the arm. Bareheaded and wreathed in smiles, the two stood for a moment upon the balcony and bowed to the thousands of cheering people, and then they disappeared. The birthday party was over.

Just under three hours of batting by the Gentlemen had produced a memorable card for the crowd to mull over as it made its way home:

A. C. MacLaren		b J. T. Hearne	10
A. E. Stoddart	c Tunnicliffe	b Lockwood	4
F. S. Jackson		b J. T. Hearne	33
S. M. J. Woods		b J. T. Hearne	9
Captain E. G. Wynyard		b J. T. Hearne	0
J. R. Mason		b Lockwood	0
C. L. Townsend	c Tunnicliffe	b J. T. Hearne	17

J. A. Dixon		b Haigh	4
W. G. Grace	not out		31
G. MacGregor		b J. T. Hearne	1
C. J. Kortright	c Haigh	b Lockwood	46
	Byes 2, leg bye 1		3
		Total	158

Fall of Wickets:
1/5; 2/41; 3/55; 4/55; 5/56; 6/56; 7/77; 8/77; 9/80

	O	M	R	W
Lockwood	20.3	6	39	3
J. T. Hearne	27	10	65	6
Haigh	10	1	21	1
A. Hearne	4	1	9	0
Storer	2	0	10	0
Brockwell	6	2	7	0
Abel	2	1	4	0

The mood of the critics at the end of the day was mixed. There was disappointment about the batting of most of the amateurs and some frustration that Kortright, perhaps seduced by the prospect of his half-century, had not been able to restrain himself for just a few more minutes; but such feelings were more than outweighed by an acceptance that the better team had won (whatever the Gentlemen's ill luck with the weather), pride in the injured WG's valiant innings, and above all intense satisfaction that the match, instead of ending tamely, had produced such a wonderfully dramatic finish – the most exciting in the annual encounter at Lord's since W. S. Patterson and poor Fred

Grace had brought the Gentlemen home in 1877 by putting on 46 for the last wicket. Granted all of which, it seemed distinctly curmudgeonly to complain overmuch about the embarrassing collapse, without which there would have been no thrilling finale and Kortright's fateful rush of blood at the death.

Not everyone, however, was satisfied by the three days of cricket. 'Man of Kent', writing to the *Sportsman* soon after the match finished, asserted strongly that too much time had been wasted and that the Pavilion had been full of remarks like 'waste of time for tea', 'twenty minutes for a photograph', and 'drawing at 6.30 instead of 7'. His particular grievance concerned trial balls, of which in the match he had counted well over 150, resulting he computed in a gross waste of just over half an hour. Perhaps he had a point; yet the fact was that in the course of the match 426.3 overs were bowled at an average of just under 25 overs per hour. Admittedly these were five-ball overs, but viewed through latter-day eyes it was still an impressively brisk rate. Despite Kortright's lengthy run-up the Gentlemen bowled their overs rather quicker than the Players. The other finding to be gleaned from a modest exercise in number-crunching is that the Gentlemen scored their runs at a rate of just under 61 runs per hour, which is about what one would expect, but that the Players scored theirs at a little over 62 rph, which is less predictable. Of course the wicket and match situation did not remain uniform; nevertheless, these one-off figures do suggest that the stereotyped contrast between amateur dash and professional plod is perhaps exaggerated.

Yet these three days transcended any set of statistics, for virtually all who saw WG's jubilee match were certain that it would abide forever in the memory. 'One of the most remarkable matches witnessed on the historic Lord's ground,' declared the *Sportsman*, and the *Daily Telegraph* agreed: 'By general consent the match was one of the best ever seen at Lord's. In every way the display of cricket was exceptional – batting, bowling, and fielding of the very highest class being shown.' The *Daily News* put it best of all: 'Everyone seemed to feel the importance of the occasion and in the atmosphere of the game from first to last there was something electrical.' Almost a century later it is possible to savour only something of that atmosphere, but enough to appreciate that it was indeed a very special episode in cricketing history. It is hard not to feel that the match also had a peculiarly archetypal resolution: the Players won, but the Gentlemen took the glory. Ever thus, it seemingly would be.

7

After the Party

E VEN AS THE verdicts on his great match were being sent down the wires, WG had caught an evening train to Nottingham. The next morning at Trent Bridge he opened the batting for his county and, though getting ever lamer, occupied the crease for the entire day, scoring 143 not out. On the Friday he was finally dismissed for 168, an encouraging start to post-jubilee life. Over the ensuing weeks several of his fellow participants prospered with the bat. Stoddart had a run of good scores; Gunn took an unbeaten 236 off the Surrey attack at the Oval; Abel found that there were indeed other bowlers than Kortright from whom to score runs; and Tunnicliffe, batting with J. T. Brown at Chesterfield, put on a record 554 for the first wicket. It was all the more remarkable a performance on Tunnicliffe's part because, following a series of mishaps, he had had no food since the previous teatime and had sat up all night at a dirty inn rather than risk a damp bed. Shrewsbury, after his failures at Lord's, returned to form and also took the time to plan his summer holiday in Hastings: 'I want a nice quiet place, where there are not a lot of people staying and where the apartments and cooking are good.' WG himself could not quite keep up his marvellous form of mid-July, but did score an excellent

93 against Sussex before surprising everyone by declaring while he was still at the crease: it transpired that that was the only score under a hundred that he had not made in his first-class career. Inevitably the rush of events meant that immediate memories of those three celebratory days at Lord's tended to fade, but it was a fitting gesture when towards the end of the season MCC presented a suitably inscribed medal to each cricketer who had taken part in the match.

The winter of 1898–9 was not a happy time for WG. His favourite child and only daughter, Bessie, died of typhoid at the age of twenty. He was also under pressure from his publisher to complete the book of reminiscences that was supposed to have been ready for his jubilee season. A journalist, Arthur Porritt, was called in to help with the task. Porritt found it a singularly frustrating exercise, as when he tried in vain to draw out WG about what it felt like to play a big innings in a major match: 'I did not feel anything; I had too much to do to watch the bowling and see how the fieldsmen were moved about to think of anything.' WG's main worry, Porritt later recalled, was that his ghost might employ words that he himself would not have dreamt of using, and going through a draft chapter one day he objected to 'inimical': ' "No," he said firmly, "that word can't go in. Why, if that went into the book I should have the fellows at Lord's coming to me in the Pavilion and saying, 'Look here, WG, where did you get that word from?' " ' Eventually a rather tame book was produced, revealing disappointingly little about the man and his life.

The next summer, the last of the old century, marked a watershed in WG's career. During May he played four games for

Gloucestershire, but then resigned the captaincy and no longer appeared in the team. The reason was that he had accepted an offer of £600 a year to manage and captain the new London County club that was to be based at the Crystal Palace. He apparently believed that his new post was compatible with continuing to appear for Gloucestershire, but the county committee did not agree and his departure was acrimonious. WG was perhaps happy to move to London and start a new life after his daughter's death. Early in June he played at Trent Bridge against Australia in what was to be his last test: his batting was still up to standard, and he bowled over twenty overs in the match, but his fielding was becoming a liability. A few weeks later it was on to Lord's, where he retained the captaincy of the Gentlemen. It was possibly on this occasion that he was filmed practising in the nets: there is little footwork but complete certainty, and almost every ball meets the middle of the bat. In the match itself, going in at number seven, he batted finely for 78 before being run out by his partner Mason, who foolishly called for a quick single to mid-off, forgetting WG's size and age. When the Players batted MacLaren took two marvellous catches in the deep off Jephson, and after one of them WG lumbered over to deep square leg to shake his hand, crying 'You caught it finely, Archie.' The Gentlemen won by an innings and thus avenged the previous year's defeat.

Certainly there were plenty of runs about – some thought too many – during 1899. Somerset under the indomitable captaincy of Sammy Woods seemed to be on the receiving end of most of them, as Abel carried his bat for 357 at the Oval, while at Taunton, in the greatest of all military partnerships, Wynyard put on 411 for the sixth wicket with Major R. M. Poore. Against rather better bowling Alec Hearne and Mason made an undefeated stand of 321 at Trent Bridge. Missing out on all these run feasts was Stoddart, who now more or less dropped out of the first-class game, apparently having no heart for it; though it was typical that when the schoolboy Collins scored 628 not out at Clifton College to break his record, 'Stoddy' presented him with a bat.

But for all the striking statistics the main focus of the summer was on the test series, which following Lord Hawke's initiative was a five-match affair. The first saw the debut of Rhodes and the finale of not only WG but also Gunn and Storer. MacLaren took over the captaincy for the rest of the series, perhaps to the disappointment of Jackson; though the Yorkshireman did have the consolation at Lord's of wearing three different caps (county, varsity and I Zingari) during a single day's play. This Second Test produced the only result of the series – a ten-wicket win for Australia – and Shrewsbury was asked to play in the third, but declined on the grounds that he was too old to take the strain. In the ensuing contest at Headingley, J. T. Hearne took one of the great hat-tricks of test match history: Clem Hill, Syd Gregory and Monty Noble, each for a duck. As usual the final test was at the Oval, where Lockwood turned in an even greater bowling performance, taking seven for 71 on the familiar adamantine wicket there. He was much annoyed not to receive any talent money for this, unlike Tom Hayward for his century in the same match. It was also here that Townsend played his second and, as it turned out, last test: so recently WG's great hope for the future, he was as a bowler a mere shadow of his former self. Yet as a batsman he had already this season done one imperishable thing, which was to be at the crease when Neville Cardus went to Old Trafford for the first time. He scored 91, and Cardus wrote over half a century later, 'I can vaguely see him now, tall when the ball was coming to him, but he bent gracefully over it as he played forward.'

Yet a game capable of producing compelling images for an impressionable ten-year-old was on the verge of a major and bitter controversy. The problem was throwing, which apart from very occasional actions by umpires had gone unchecked in English cricket for many years. By the late 1890s a shadow of suspicion lay on most of the leading bowlers of the day, including Kortright. Levi Wright later recalled the unwise words of a fellow Derbyshire batsman:

Chatterton once had the misfortune to state that Kortright threw. Whether Kortright heard him or was told about it I do not know, but when Chatterton passed Korty to join me at the wicket, Kortright said to him, 'I throw do I Chatterton, I will show you if I throw.' I think Chatty only had three balls. The first two were a bit short and whizzed past his nose, but the third was a yorker like greased lightning and the stumps were spread-eagled. Chatterton did not like Kortright after that.

It may well have been the freely circulating rumours about his action, added to a genuine leg strain, that accounted for Kortright's entire absence in 1899 from the first-class arena. That autumn MCC at last passed a new law allowing the square-leg umpire to call no-ball and the following summer umpires West and Phillips renewed their campaign, begun in 1898 but seemingly suspended. West again called Fry; while Phillips at Taunton twice no-balled Somerset's slow left-arm bowler Edwin Tyler, to the indignation of not only Woods but also the other umpire, who showed what he thought of it by refusing to add extra balls to the over. Phillips in 1900 also called Lancashire's Arthur Mold, the most notorious chucker of the past decade. That December there was a meeting at Lord's of the county captains, of whom only MacLaren of Lancashire declined to endorse Phillips. The decisive shoot-out came in 1901. After his fellow umpires had chickened out of no-balling Mold during the early part of the season, Phillips at last stood at Old Trafford and, by calling him sixteen times in ten overs, effectively ended his career. Thereafter the problem sharply receded, as county captains declined to countenance in their teams bowlers with doubtful actions. Among those affected was Kortright, who had returned for Essex in 1900 but subsequently hardly bowled fast again in county cricket, though he still had the capacity. As for Phillips, after this important display of courage and obstinacy, he began to be regarded as something of a Pooh-Bah in the cricket world and perhaps swelled in his own estimation; but he continued to study his algebra and after a few more seasons duly left cricket to begin a career in North America as a mining engineer.

By the new century several other of the Gentlemen of '98 besides Kortright were becoming only intermittent presences in first-class cricket. Stoddart's last appearance for Middlesex was in 1900, on the occasion of J. T. Hearne's benefit, and he bowed out with 221 against the inevitable Somerset; Dixon relinquished the Notts captaincy; Townsend qualified as a solicitor; Jackson went to the Boer War; and Wynyard became instructor in military engineering at Sandhurst, where at one match when WG was due to bring a team but had to drop out he successfully passed himself off as the great man (beard, voice, batting style and all), to the subsequent amusement of the cadets and annoyance of the commandant. WG himself was also missing from Gentlemen and Players at Lord's in 1900. He was in fair form and would like to have played, but it seems that MCC were not greatly enamoured of the London County venture. Captain in his place was Woods, who acted characteristically at the end of an epic contest. The Players had been set over 500 to win and the scores were level with eight wickets down when stumps were supposed to be drawn. 'Play it out!' cried the spectators. The umpires (one of whom was Phillips) looked to Woods. He took the ball, and Rhodes made the winning hit. Would the deposed WG have done the same? Probably not, though he would have relished the situation. Over the next few years, though never again playing for the Gentlemen at Lord's, he showed himself still capable of some fine performances, none more so than when he took five for 29 against the Australians on a good wicket in 1902. These were the Australians, immortalised by Victor Trumper's presence, who at Old Trafford won the most compelling of tests by three runs, the decisive result of the series and one that caused infinite pain to MacLaren as England's captain. There was much criticism of his handling of the team; but in truth he had been undone by the chairman of the selectors, Lord Hawke, who was more concerned with the well-being of Yorkshire than England. 'My God, look what they've given me! Do they think we're playing the blind asylum?' exploded MacLaren when he was shown the team list.

Almost but not quite saving the home side on that memorable occasion was Lockwood. A few weeks earlier he had scored a century for the Players at Lord's and now at Old Trafford he produced some inspired bowling, returning match figures of eleven for 76. Yet as four seasons earlier it was a surprise in 1902 that he was playing first-class cricket at all. Once again the story involved the liquor factor, against a background in 1901 of rumbling doubts about the legitimacy of his bowling action and, probably more important to Lockwood, a benefit match completely ruined by rain. The Surrey committee once more treated him with commendable sense, by dropping him from the side, arranging for Yorkshire to play an additional benefit match on his behalf, and only re-engaging him on condition that he again took the pledge. The benefit yielded £1,000, most of which the committee invested on the player's behalf (following the Yorkshire example) in Mexican Railways debenture stock. Lockwood was thus guaranteed an income after his playing days were over; and his superb performances in 1902 were just reward for the committee's handling of him. It was a pity that Surrey had not adopted this investment policy earlier, for the previous beneficiary, Brockwell, had netted some £500 in 1900 and proceeded to spend, spend, spend as if there were no tomorrow, even though his cricketing form was manifestly in decline. He was not called 'Band-box Brockwell' for nothing.

Someone who still watched the pennies, even though he had little need to, was Arthur Shrewsbury, whose sports equipment concern was quietly prospering by the turn of the century.

'My management of my business affairs during my life time has placed me in a position I am proud of,' he boasted in 1900 to his partner Alfred Shaw. He also continued to play for his county (though never again for the Players at Lord's) and in 1902 was, according to *Wisden*, 'as patient and watchful as ever'. But that autumn Shrewsbury began to complain of kidney pains and found walking difficult. In February he spent some time in a London nursing home, where the specialists were unable to find anything seriously the matter with him. He returned to Nottingham and went to convalesce at his sister's home in Gedling, a few miles outside the city. There he seemed to be making good progress, but on a Tuesday evening in May, shortly after calling for a cup of cocoa, he shot himself first in the chest and then, fatally, in the head. He was forty-seven. In a remarkably speedy inquest, coroner and jury agreed the next day that Shrewsbury's mind had been unhinged by the belief, for which there was no evidence, that he had an incurable disease. The news came as a terrible shock to those who knew him, though not as a complete surprise; and the Notts secretary, Harry Turner, remarked that Shrewsbury had recently begun to complain of pains in the head and could not bear anyone in the same room as himself to laugh. The county itself was playing at Hove, scene of some of Shrewsbury's greatest innings; and the third day was abandoned with the younger Notts players in a state of distress, Tom Wass crying like a child and refusing to be consoled. William Gunn was less unmanned, but told a journalist that the news was the most painful he had ever experienced. The funeral took place at Gedling on the Friday, 'the sun shining brilliantly in a cloud-flecked sky of summer blue', the

Nottingham Daily Express related, 'to the accompaniment of the sweet piping of Nature's feathered songsters'. Gunn, Dixon and Shaw were three of the many mourners. WG was not present, but some years later would pay Shrewsbury the ultimate tribute when asked with whom he would most prefer to open England's batting. He simply replied: 'Give me Arthur.'

Not least would he be remembered for his captaincy of the Players at Lord's; and in that position, the most prestigious open to a professional cricketer, he had been succeeded by Abel (four times) and Hayward. In 1904 it was the turn of Lilley, who gave such satisfaction that he received the following letter from Ranji:

> May I say how delighted I was to find how charmingly you justified your position? My admiration for you as a man increases as I see more and more of you every year. May you live long to adorn the profession which men like yourself raise yearly in the public estimation. It would afford me great pleasure to spend an evening in town with you, if you happen to be here. We can dine in company with some mutual comrades like Mr MacLaren and do a theatre . . .

Something should be allowed for the fact that Lilley's failure to enforce the follow-on had enabled the writer to make a match-winning century for the Gentlemen on the last afternoon. Nevertheless the letter was a sign that, at the very top of the game anyhow, the social gap between amateur and professional was starting to narrow. Yet overall in first-class cricket during the Edwardian period the day-to-day barriers between the two classes remained almost as strong as ever; it was still virtually unthinkable that a middle-class gentleman unable to afford to play cricket for fun should turn professional; and Shrewsbury from his far pavilion would have nodded knowingly at Albert Knight's robust assertion in 1906 that 'the salaried amateur is far more adequately remunerated than a professional of purely equal skill.' Moreover, there still obtained the stylistic divide – usually implicit, occasionally explicit. The Sussex professional Joe Vine was a natural hitter, but when he opened the batting with Fry he was forbidden to hit more than one boundary an over. Vine would recall: 'I once hit three fours in the same over, and Mr Fry came up to me and told me plainly that it was my job to stay there, and leave that sort of cricket to him.' Very splendid that cricket could be too, never more so than in 1903 when Fry and MacLaren for the Gentlemen at Lord's put on 309 in less than three hours, prompting Cardus to write in later years that 'never has such batsmanship been seen as this for opulence and prerogative'. Yet of the fourteen encounters between 1901 and 1914, the Players won seven and the Gentlemen only four, demonstrating once again that fine cover-drives do not always butter the parsnips.

Inevitably the members of the victorious Players' team of 1898 began to drop out of the first-class game, including all three Surrey representatives. Brockwell retired in 1903 and lived prosperously enough at Ham, but in 1912 was much affected by the death of his close friend Tom Richardson and took to drink. Lockwood's last season was 1904 and soon afterwards he moved back to Nottingham, from where he intimidated a new generation of cricketers by taking on the occasional coaching engagement. Eye trouble brought Abel's career to an end, also in 1904, and he concentrated on his modestly successful sports equipment business hard by the Oval. In 1908 *The Times*, in a piece about Saturday afternoon cricket, reported that 'the Cockney legend that Abel got most of his runs by a kind of cunning coping still survives in the parks'; while a few years later the man himself went temporarily into hiding because of his resemblance to the wanted Dr Crippen. Gunn also retired in 1904 and, following Shrewsbury's suicide, this brought an era in professional batting unmistakably to a close. He likewise concentrated on his own rather more flourishing business and became a very model of the strict, paternalist employer, dark-suited and utterly regular in his working habits. The two members of the eleven who never played for England followed each other in quick succession: Alec Hearne, troubled by lameness, in 1906, subsequently becoming the idolised coach at Dulwich College; and Tunnicliffe in 1907, going as coach to Clifton College, where he was able to continue to live out his maxim that 'cricket and religion go together'.

Lilley meanwhile continued to keep wicket for England through the 1900s, even after he had become a grandfather. He was troubled by varicose veins, but his hands remained injury-free and indeed showed few signs of his occupation. The end of his career came abruptly towards the close of the 1911 season and was due to the habit he had increasingly fallen into of ordering everyone about the field, often so loudly that the crowd could hear him. In a match at Harrogate his captain, F. R. Foster, told him to mind his own business; after lunch there was dead silence in the professionals' dressing room when Foster arrived to lead them out; and Lilley was dropped, just weeks before Warwickshire won the county championship for the first time. But at least he had easily seen off his long-time rival, Bill Storer, who had retired in 1905 because of ill health. He lived only seven more years and died of dropsy at his home in Derby, aged forty-four. That left two bowlers still playing. Haigh lasted until 1913 and then became coach at Winchester College, having ten times headed his county's bowling averages and been, in Old Ebor's phrase, 'for eighteen years the sunshine of the Yorkshire eleven'. Only J. T. Hearne, by now known as 'Tireless' to his fellow pros, went on, recovering from a bad season in 1909 that had seemed to spell the end. He was the ultimate senior pro, above all (as Harry Lee recalled) when Middlesex played away and the professionals stayed in their separate hotel:

> J. T. set the hour for us to be at meals or in bed. When we came to sit down, the juniors stood back until the seniors had chosen their places. Then J. T. would take his seat at the head of the table and carve the joint, handing round the plates in proper order of seniority, and giving himself the carver's portion last of all.

By 1914 he had taken over 3,000 wickets, more than anyone else in the game, and truly earned his plate of meat.

None of the amateur counterparts kept going that long, at least on a daily basis. Townsend, as lamp-post like as ever and practising as a solicitor in Stockton-on-Tees, played most of his cricket in the local league, where a spectator amused the rest of the ring by observing that 'Yon lad hasn't enough fat on him to grease a gimlet.' Also qualified as a solicitor was Mason, who gave up the Kent captaincy from 1903 and thereafter played only half seasons. But he topped the national batting averages in 1909 and on his marriage three years later was presented by Kentish admirers with a silver tray and candelabra. Kortright captained Essex in 1903, employing himself mainly as a batsman, and then virtually abandoned the first-class scene. He returned with relief to minor cricket, where no umpire would dare to no-ball him, and playing at Winchester College in 1907 for A. J. Webbe's XI showed himself still capable of bowling a ball that soared over the wicket-keeper's head for six byes. As for his two opening partners, Jackson enjoyed a golden summer in 1905 as England's captain and skippered the Gentlemen to victory at Lord's in 1906 before playing his last match for Yorkshire the following summer; and Woods too retired in 1907, but remained as Somerset's secretary and over the ensuing years became an even greater, more popular local character than he had been before. His fund of anecdotes was limitless, he called everyone 'me dear', he sang in all the village concerts round Taunton and Bridgwater, and one of his greatest pleasures was amazing friends by digging up bottles of beer that he had hidden in countryside ditches the night before.

Wynyard fully shared the love of a practical joke, but preferred to play on a wider stage, seemingly treating himself to a global cricket tour after he had retired from the Army in 1903. Thus in 1904–5 he went to the West Indies under Lord Brackley and topped the averages; the next winter he was in South Africa under Plum Warner and played two tests, but suffered from ill health; twelve months later he was captaining the MCC team to New Zealand, where he snapped a tendon in the third match and had to return home; undeterred, he went to North America in the autumn of 1907 and made a big century on Staten Island; March 1909 saw him in Egypt, where he scored a half-century at Cairo; and finally, or so it seemed, he was back in South Africa in 1909–10 under H. D. G. Leveson Gower. By contrast MacGregor preferred to stay at home and concentrate on his Stock Exchange business, giving up after 1907 the Middlesex captaincy he had inherited from Stoddart. What may have prompted that decision was an unpleasant row with MacLaren during the match with Lancashire at Lord's. Essentially what happened was that, following rain, MacLaren refused to go on with the game because some disgruntled spectators had walked on the wicket, even though they had scarcely damaged it. MacGregor was dismayed and almost everyone (including WG in the *Morning Post*) condemned the Lancashire captain. MacLaren's relations with Lord's had never been easy and he once remarked that he 'always felt that he would get half a dozen if he came in at the wrong door' there. He gave up the Lancashire captaincy in 1908; the next season he ill-advisedly captained England when past his best; and after 1910 he played little first-class cricket. But he did go on Lord Hawke's tour of the Argentine in 1911–12 and began with four ducks, presumably a South American record.

What of WG? He enjoyed himself playing for London County in the early years of the century and was, as Beldam recalled, as full of his tricks as ever:

When he was bowling, just as he was about to start his run up and just as the batsman had prepared to watch him, he would stop and order short-leg to move a little this way or that, or deep long-on to move further round, and then he would proceed most likely to bowl the ball well on the off side of the wicket.

Commercially, however, the venture proved a failure and in 1905 it was wound up. WG subsequently played little first-class cricket, but in 1906 he was persuaded to play one last time in the Gentlemen and Players match at the Oval. On his fifty-eighth birthday, he delighted everyone by scoring a resolute 74 as the Gentlemen batted for a draw. 'There. I shan't play any more,' he declared after lumbering back into the dressing room and throwing his bat down on the table. He did of course continue to play, but mostly for his home team of Eltham in south-east London. He also continued to lead an intensely active life, once exhausting the much younger Gilbert Jessop by a day that comprised forty-five holes of golf in rough weather at Maidenhead, dinner in town, and a vigorous session of curl-ing at the Prince's ice-skating club before catching the last train back to the suburbs. Bowls, shooting, coursing and billiards were other favourite activities of old age, while he never lost his lifelong enthusiasm for whist, virtually the only subject he ever professed to read a book about. He was also an occasional figure at Lord's, to be seen on big-match days on one of the lower seats of the Pavilion with a friend on either side. No doubt he was there in July 1914 when, with West one of the umpires, the Gentlemen surprised many by winning a grand match against a very strong Players team. Less than a fortnight later, on Saturday the 25th, he was playing for Eltham at Grove Park. In a drawn game, Eltham were in some trouble at 31 for four, but WG came in and scored 69 not out. According to the *Eltham and District Times*, its brief report concealed in a mass of local scores, 'he got his runs all round the wicket, being especially strong on the off side.' Suitably undefeated, it turned out to be the final innings of WG's fifty-eighth consecutive season and the last he ever played.

When war broke out soon afterwards, opinion was divided as to whether the county programme should continue. Many of the professionals, mindful of their match fees, were in favour, including J. T. Hearne. But on August the 27th, in a letter to the *Sportsman*, WG made a decisive intervention:

> The fighting on the Continent is very severe, and will probably be prolonged. I think the time has arrived when the county cricket season should be closed, for it is not fitting at a time like the present that able-bodied men should play day after day and pleasure-seekers look on. There are so many who are young and able, and yet are hanging back. I should like to see all first-class cricketers of suitable age, etc, set a good example, and come to the help of their country without delay in its hour of need.

WG's letter has been dismissed, with the enormous condescension of posterity, as 'a pathetic attempt by the Doctor to interfere in matters so tragically beyond his comprehension': yet he foresaw, when many did not, that the conflict would be protracted and his call to put away bat and ball revealed him in harmony with the national mood. He himself was too old to put on khaki, but several of his former colleagues relished the prospect: Wynyard returned to the fold and took on a series of staff appointments; MacLaren enlisted in October, spending most of the war recruiting in the Manchester area; and Jackson raised and commanded his own West Yorkshire Regiment battalion. No response was more action-seeking than that of Woods, who at the age of forty-six found it difficult to enlist but eventually secured a berth with the 6th Somersets. There followed some excitements in and around Khartoum before malaria ended his adventure. 'The most overrated stretch of water in existence,' he would later call the Nile, before going on in a style curiously reminiscent of Bertie Wooster: 'Why one is called the Blue Nile and the other the White Nile is a mystery. They are both yellow or brown streams. Still people flock from America every winter and go in the shade to see the sights. Nothing better to do, I suppose!'

For WG's vice-captain, however, the outbreak of war and appalling loss of life were the last straw. 'That Son of Grief', the poet Francis Thompson had called 'Drew' Stoddart back in 1898 (in a review of Housman's *A Shropshire Lad*), and so it proved. The Edwardian years were a depressing struggle for this most beloved of cricketers. Having left the Stock Exchange, he had sinecure posts at the Queen's Club and, supreme bathos, Neasden Golf Club; and though he enjoyed playing golf himself, he came to regard it as wasted time, saying that it had deprived him of several years of what should have been active athletic life. By the first winter of war he was suffering from poor nerves, financial problems and a loveless marriage. The end came on Easter Saturday 1915, when at the age of fifty-two he shot himself through the head at his home in Maida Vale. 'Lately he had been forgetful and irritable, and even when she had rustled a paper he had asked her not to do so, saying it would drive him mad,' Mrs Ethel Stoddart told the inquest. The sporting world was profoundly shaken. In the eloquent under-statement of the *Pall Mall Gazette*: 'It is all too sad for words.' Stoddart's ashes were buried in his mother's grave at Coventry, but the funeral took place at Golders Green. J. T. Hearne was among those present and his wreath was inscribed 'In fond and grateful memory of my old captain'.

Nor was WG long for this world. In September 1915, work-ing in his garden at home, he suffered a stroke. He recovered, but soon afterwards was much upset by the first Zeppelin raid, some of whose bombs dropped in south-east London. Leveson Gower tried to cheer him up with some well-intentioned chaff. 'How can you mind the Zepps, WG, you who have played all the fastest bowlers of your time?' 'Ah, but I could see those beggars. I can't see these.' There quickly followed two more strokes, the second of which, on October the 23rd, was fatal. It was a Saturday and WG was sixty-seven. Inevitably there was a widespread sense of grief and loss when the news became known, yet to read the newspapers of the days that followed is to be reminded that there was a great and difficult war going on and that the recent brutal killing of Nurse Edith Cavell seemed in most eyes the more important event. WG's funeral took place on the Tuesday at Elmer's End Cemetery in Beckenham; and among the congregation, far less big than it would have been in peacetime, were Townsend as well as MacLaren, Mason, MacGregor and Alec Hearne. The next day there was published

George V's solemn appeal: 'At this grave moment in the struggle between my people and a highly organised enemy who has Transgressed the Laws of Nations', the King called on his subjects 'to come forward voluntarily and take your share in the fight'. Altogether it was a strangely muted end to the life of one who had figured so large in the national consciousness for so long; but in the context WG perhaps would not have minded.

Four years later, in the summer of 1919 with the war safely won, there was published under MCC's auspices *The Memorial Biography of Dr W. G. Grace* and full justice was done. Also concerned to set the record straight was MacLaren, who at about this time wrote an extraordinarily long letter to *The Times* justifying in exhaustive detail his tactics in the Old Trafford test of 1902. The first post-war tourists were the Australian Imperial Forces and their opening match was at Old Buckenham Hall in Norfolk against Lionel Robinson's eleven. Mason captained it and, in his last first-class innings, scored 18 batting at number ten. It should have been a happy summer of peace, but in August 1919, just before his fiftieth birthday, Gregor MacGregor died of heart failure in a London nursing home. He had recently taken his son to public schools' week at Lord's and been delighted to meet Percy Chapman, the crack cricketer from his old school. The next year saw contrasting fortunes for two of the pros: Brockwell, never a member of the Cricketers' Fund Friendly Society, had fallen on hard times and an appeal on his behalf appeared in the *Sporting Life*; but J. T. Hearne, having virtually retired, was elected to the Middlesex committee, only the second professional to be so honoured, the first being Gunn for Nottinghamshire before the war. Billy Gunn himself died in January 1921 and left almost £60,000. He was followed a few weeks later by Schofield Haigh, who left rather less; and when his widow applied to Yorkshire for £250 from his benefit money in order to buy a cottage, the club refused and instead lent her the money, on which she had to pay interest.

During these early post-war years the different cricketing generations did not always rub shoulders easily. Tunnicliffe had as his assistant in 1921 the young Walter Hammond and gave him much old-school advice, sometimes not appreciated, about both technique and comportment. That same summer Abel sat in the Oval pavilion and shook his head sadly at the successes of the Australian fast bowlers. 'Oh yes, Bobby,' said one of the batsmen, '*you* never ran away from fast bowling, did you? There was once a man called Kortright.' 'Well,' replied the little man, still wearing his faded chocolate cap, 'perhaps I did. But I'll tell you the difference between you and me. I used to leave my bat behind, you take yours with you.' Typically impatient of the general tide of criticism that summer was Woods, who penned a brisk letter to *The Times*: 'The England selectors have a difficult task to pick their side; this is not made any easier by people writing to the papers and giving their ideas of the team that should be picked, and also writing as to how to play fast bowling and how not to.' One man who very much had his own ideas about how to beat the Australians was MacLaren, who throughout the summer argued forcibly that they would be vulnerable to a zestful, keen-fielding, mostly young and defi-nitely all-amateur team. Almost right at the end, at Eastbourne, he got his chance and captained his carefully-chosen team to a marvellous, improbable victory after they had been bowled out for 43 on the first morning. 'The noblest Roman of them all', as Cardus would call him, remained calm and imperturbable throughout.

There were some last flurries of action left. Townsend in 1922 played three final matches for Gloucestershire. He was bowled cheaply by Rhodes at Bristol, but a 61 at Leyton 'revived pleasant memories', in the apt words of *Wisden*. The following winter MacLaren took an MCC team to New Zealand and at the age of fifty-one scored a majestic 200 not out against the host country at the Basin Reserve in Wellington. It turned out to be his first-class swansong, for later in the match he ricked his knee and did not play again on the tour. But perhaps appropriately it fell to J. T. Hearne to make the last first-class appearance of any of the twenty-two. He was included in the Middlesex side that played in 1923 against Scotland in Edinburgh, where the team was well entertained and 'JT' drank a cocktail for the first time in his life; while on the field of play he scored 20 and took six wickets. However, mention must be made of Wynyard, still going gamely. A few weeks later he captained the party of Free Foresters that toured Canada, where in Toronto his lobs so baffled XVIII of Public Schools that he finished with five for 10. Meanwhile, back in north-west London, the Grace Gates had recently been erected at Lord's, amidst much discussion about the wording under Grace's name. Suggestions in English, in Latin and even in Greek were put forward, but no one could agree. At last they called on Jackson, whose political career was by now so flourishing that he became that year chairman of the Conservative Party. 'Why not simply "The great Cricketer"?' he said, and so it was.

English cricket in general between the wars was marked by continuity, with Lord Harris (until his death in 1932) and Plum Warner as the powerful twin bastions of pre-1914 values. The captaincy of England and the counties remained firmly in amateur hands, so much so that Hammond had to change status from professional to amateur in order to lead his country; while when Leicestershire out of necessity in 1935 appointed as captain the professional all-rounder Ewart Astill, he was replaced after one season even though he had taken the county to its highest position in the championship since the war. Gentlemen and Players at Lord's continued as an attractive, competitive fixture, though the Gentlemen won only twice in the whole period, reflecting the way in which changed socio-economic conditions were diminishing the supply of high-class amateurs to the game. Shamateurism inevitably became even more widespread and blatant, while for the professionals it was still on the whole payment by match supplemented by talent money, a formula for caution and insecurity. 'That's another bag of coal for the winter,' Hampshire's Phil Mead would famously mutter as he turned one past short leg to reach yet another half-century. Conditions in the professionals' dressing rooms were still poor: at Worcester the gaps in the floorboards were notorious and at Bournemouth the accommodation was akin to a cowshed. Segregation remained the order of the day, though Surrey's Percy Fender, an iconoclast among captains, insisted on leading his whole team out together, even when playing away to Middlesex. Lord Harris was not amused: 'It may be all right at the Oval, Fender, but we don't do that kind of thing at Lord's.' Interestingly, when Fender also attempted to have his team all changing together, the person who successfully resisted this move was his senior professional, Jack Hobbs. The reason he gave was that the pros all liked to have a good moan about their captain at the end of the day. As in an earlier age the professionals of this period mostly accepted the flamboyant amateurs as part of the natural order of things, but just occasionally they would get in an effective dig. One such moment occurred on a muddy wicket at Derby in the 1930s. The batsman was the Middlesex captain Walter Robins, who loved to charge down the pitch to slow bowlers; and if he missed the ball he would simply keep going towards the pavilion. On this day he duly charged and missed and was on his way, only for Patsy Hendren at the non-striker's end to shout 'He's missed it!' Robins turned and dived into the dirt; but as he got up, feeling rather pleased with himself, he saw that the bails were off and that the wicket-keeper was in the middle of a leisurely chat with first slip. It was a vignette that embodied much social history.

One of the victims of the Harris autocracy was Bill West. Umpiring Gentlemen and Players at Lord's in 1925 he mistakenly gave Gubby Allen out; the batsman on returning to the Pavilion was asked by Harris if he was satisfied with the decision; Allen said he was not; and Harris had West struck off the first-class list. It was a harsh end to a long umpiring career. West lived until 1938, eight years after the death in Vancouver of his old colleague Jim Phillips. By the 1930s there were cricketing berths for the reliable, long-lived Hearnes – Alec as Kent scorer, JT coaching at Oxford University – but most of the other professionals were fading away. Dick Lilley had already died, in 1929 near Bristol, where he had run a hotel after his playing

days. Next to go, after what *Wisden* with masterly understate-
ment called 'a somewhat chequered career', was Bill Lockwood
in 1932. Confined to a bath chair towards the end of his life, he
was to be seen near the sight-screen at Trent Bridge, where he
thought highly of the young Harold Larwood. 'If the lad were
only an inch or two taller I would not know a better,' he told
a local journalist. In a final gesture of obstinacy he refused in
1931 to go into a sanatorium after his lungs had haemorrhaged.
Lockwood's two county colleagues lived a few more years,
though both in rather sad circumstances. Bobby Abel's business had gone bankrupt in the mid-1920s and he had had to be
rescued by a *Daily Mail* fund, while in his last few years he was
completely blind, though cheerful enough. He died in 1936, a
year after the genuinely tragic figure of his old opening partner
Billy Brockwell. The *Sporting Life*'s appeal did not prove enough
and 'Brocky' during the last fifteen years of his life found himself
a member of society's underclass. He had occasional jobs, but
they rarely lasted, and for some time he was living in a partially
roofless hovel on Sundridge Park golf course. Usually he was
in and around Richmond, gathering firewood in the park and
lodging where he could. In June 1935 he was taken seriously ill
after being caught in a thunderstorm; and five days later he died
in the local infirmary. At the funeral at Richmond Cemetery
the only professional cricketer present was the ever-faithful Jack
Hearne.

Would the news of Brockwell's decline and death have
impinged on Mason, practising as a solicitor in Beckenham? Or
on Townsend, by now the official receiver for Middlesbrough
and Stockton? Probably only as a brief item in the national press.

Rather nearer the centre of cricketing power was Jackson, who during a stint as Governor of Bengal had survived an assassination attempt with what he called 'the quickest duck I ever made in my life'. Back in England he became a familiar sight demonstrating strokes to schoolboys with a beautifully rolled umbrella, whilst in 1936 he insisted that the selection committee on the forthcoming tour of Australia should not include any professionals. Experiencing an altogether less august time was his fellow old Harrovian. MacLaren's finances had always been parlous and during the inter-war years he tried – Ukridge-style – many and diverse commercial ventures, none of which remotely worked out. He was ever short of the ready and had few scruples about the niceties of debt repayment. But he never lost his confidence or his sense of the past: in his many different homes the photograph of the Gentlemen's team of 1898 was always in pride of place. A particular pleasure occurred in 1935, when he gave a talk on the wireless about WG and was able to dwell on the Old Man's innings on the second morning of his jubilee match: 'That feat has always remained in my memory. It was probably the best performance of any batsman I ever saw – taking into consideration the state of the wicket and the age of the man, to say nothing of the fact that he was playing against a very fine side.'

Three more of MacLaren's erstwhile colleagues died during these years, none so lamented as Sammy Woods in 1931. 'A Town in Mourning' was the headline of the *Taunton Courier* reporting his funeral, when hundreds stood outside the church despite heavy rain. Johnny Dixon died the same year and was remembered in Nottingham as a prominent and kindly

figure. The third was Major Teddy Wynyard, at his home at
Beaconsfield in 1936. He and Abel had paraded alongside each
other before the cinematograph; now they died within a few
weeks of each other; but in their lives as a whole they had had
precious little in common. Meanwhile, seemingly impervious
to death and decay, Kortright continued to stride round the
Essex countryside shooting pheasants and playing golf. In the
first half of the 1930s, in his early sixties, he even played four
seasons of village cricket, bowling at a fairly brisk pace. It was
at about this time that he met Charles Tennyson, grandson of
the poet and present as a young man at Lord's in July 1898.
Tennyson reminded him of the final afternoon and charged
him with having succumbed to the ambition of making fifty
in a Gentlemen and Players match – an intrepid accusation that
Kortright repudiated indignantly, saying that such a thing had
never crossed his mind for a moment.

On the day that Hitler invaded Poland in 1939, Neville
Cardus was in the Long Room at Lord's. Suddenly two work-
men entered, took down the bust of WG, and carried it away in a
bag. 'Did you see, sir?' a finely preserved member with spats and
rolled umbrella asked Cardus. He told him he had seen. 'That
means war,' the member said. Over the next six years Lord's
was lucky enough to escape major damage; though Tunnicliffe
in Bristol had a close shave when his home was bombed and he
was only hauled out of the debris after several hours. During
the war the mood of the country became palpably more egali-
tarian and in *Wisden* in 1943 R. C. Robertson-Glasgow, the
Somerset amateur and inimitable cricket writer, argued that it
was time to end the two-class system, asserting that 'the hour is

ripe, indeed over-ripe, for the sweeping away of anachronisms and the exploding of humbug.' A central plank of his case was that the majority of so-called amateurs, though loving the game, 'play it for the equivalent of money, namely for the publicity which attracts clients to themselves or to the business for which they may be working'. But it was a premature call, for when the following spring an MCC select committee under Jackson's chairmanship reported on what the post-war shape of the game should be, there were no qualms expressed about maintaining the distinction.

Soon afterwards, in April 1944, a pillar of the traditional system, Jack Hearne, died at his home in Chalfont St Giles. 'I have had a happy life,' he said more than once towards the end, 'and if I had to live it over again I would not choose that it should be in any way different.' At his memorial service in the parish church, where he had been the rector's warden for many years, a collection was taken for the Cricketers' Fund Friendly Society and raised over a hundred pounds. The man whom he had induced to play on almost half a century before also died in 1944. Until becoming ill, Archie MacLaren had had a good war: his wife's financial boat had at last come in and he much enjoyed telling people about how Winston Churchill had been his fag at Harrow.

County cricket resumed in 1946, a year after Labour's land-slide election victory, and all but one of the seventeen captains were amateurs. Gentlemen versus Players at Lord's also resumed and in 1948 there was a rather special encounter, on the occasion of the centenary of WG's birth. The captains were Norman Yardley and Len Hutton, and before the match began MCC's president, Lord Cornwallis, had a quiet word with them: 'This game is being downgraded and seen as a bit of a beanfeast. I hope I can count on you to restore it to its rightful place in the cricket calendar.' An excellent contest ensued and over the next few years there was some hard-fought cricket played in front of good crowds. Warner in 1950 produced his authoritative history of the fixture and in his preface invoked it as 'an historic match which began long before Test Matches were dreamed of, and which I pray, and believe, will never die out'. By the mid-1950s, however, its prestige was again in decline along with attendances, partly because of the Gentlemen's inability to win, the only post-war exception being in the extraordinary sporting summer of 1953. The problem of course was the ever-harder one, in a context of high taxation, death duties and so on, of attracting talent from the right social background. Shamateurism, increasingly more sophisticated, did its best; but by now many of the amateurs themselves heartily disliked the hypocrisy involved, perhaps especially as the barriers were starting to come down, epitomised by Hutton's appointment in 1952 as England's first professional captain. In 1957–8 a special sub-committee under the chairmanship of MCC's president, the Duke of Norfolk, considered the whole question of amateur status; but it decided that far from being obsolete, it was 'of great value to the game and should be preserved'. Soon afterwards Jim Laker (who had always disliked Gentlemen versus Players and avoided the match whenever possible) gave Gubby Allen, chairman of the England selectors, a bad quarter of an hour. He told him that he was considering becoming an amateur and, when asked why, the hard-headed Yorkshireman explained that on the impending tour of Australia he could earn more through expenses than by drawing professional pay. In the event Laker remained a professional for the time being, but it was a piquant illustration of the absurdity of the system.

All this was more or less academic to the cricketers of the Golden Age. Sir Stanley Jackson died in March 1947, John Tunnicliffe at Bristol in July 1948, a week before WG's centenary. To mark this occasion John Arlott compiled a radio feature, *The Old Man*, and one of his witnesses was Kortright. Far more loquacious than he had ever been in his playing days, he talked at some length about his part in the jubilee match and attributed his fatal last stroke not to any overwhelming ambition but to 'a fit of – what shall I say? – inferiority complex'. The next year Arlott again interviewed Kortright, who took the opportunity to tell modern-day listeners how it once was: 'To play cricket was to play a clean game, and that was always the understanding in my day that you played clean, and if anyone didn't play clean, well he heard all about it.' The straight-talking 'Korty' died in December 1952, some months after Alec Hearne. That left, for almost another six years, two last survivors; and it would, if it had been a tontine, have been a close-run thing. Jack Mason died on 15 October 1958 at his home at Cooden Beach in Sussex, where he had moved during the war. Two days later, at his home in Stockton, his fellow solicitor Charlie Townsend also crossed the bar. 'One of the greatest sporting personalities ever to have played in the North Yorkshire and South Durham Cricket League' was the extravagant tribute paid by the local press to WG's godson. It was perhaps more fitting that on the day of his death another elegant Gloucestershire batsman, Tom Graveney, was scoring a century for MCC in Perth.

It emerges from some simple arithmetic that the Gentlemen lived longer than the Players. The average longevity of the eleven amateurs was 70 years, with three (Mason, Townsend and Kortright) having become octogenarians and four (Jackson, Wynyard, MacLaren and Dixon) septuagenarians. By contrast the eleven professionals came in at an average of just under 65½ years, with only two octogenarians (Alec Hearne and Tunnicliffe) and two septuagenarians (Abel and J. T. Hearne). Only two of the amateurs (Woods and MacGregor, that hard-living Cambridge pair) died of natural causes under the age of 65, in comparison with five of the professionals (Gunn, Lockwood, Storer, Lilley and Haigh). But the senior of them all was a pro, Alec Hearne, who despite much rheumatic suffering lived to be 88. As for wealth at the time of death, the eleven Gentlemen left between them a total of £206, 253, working out at an average of £18,750 per head. The major contributors were Jackson (£85,620) and Dixon (£62,253), with Townsend managing a respectable £23,957. WG, despite a lifetime of high earnings, left a disappointing £7,278, while comprehensively bottom of the table was Woods with £137. As for the Players, it is difficult to pin down the figures for Lockwood and Brockwell, though presumably the latter had virtually nothing to leave the world. The other nine left a total of £100,415, being an average of £11,157. The lion's share was of course Gunn's (£57,392) and the only other pro in five figures was J. T. Hearne (£12,352); but all but two of the others managed four figures, the exceptions being Abel (£864) and Storer (£759). Overall, although the Gentlemen left more, as one would expect, the margin was not as great as might have been anticipated. Yet since almost all of the twenty-two were in effect paid cricketers, perhaps this was not so surprising.

For a few more years after Townsend's death amateurs and professionals continued to inhabit two separate but narrowing worlds, with no repeats of the day at Lords in 1950, as a young pro had come out to bat, that a loudspeaker announcement had solemnly corrected the scorecard: 'F. J. Titmus should, of course, read Titmus F. J.' Gentlemen still met Players at Lord's and in 1962 the captains were the appropriately contrasting pair of Ted Dexter and Fred Trueman. The match was surprisingly well attended and, as ever, fully reported. The Gentlemen batted first and scored 323, including a century from the Revd. David Sheppard and a brilliant 55 by Dexter, who 'at times was treating Trueman and Shackleton as though this was a net'. E. W. Swanton in the *Daily Telegraph* was strongly critical of Andrew for standing back to Shackleton and Walker, asserting that 'the old men would have died rather than go back to either'. The Players replied with 260 (Bailey six for 58) and on the final afternoon, after a generous declaration by Dexter, needed 29 more to win in thirty-five minutes when the rain came. Four months later, in November 1962, the Advisory County Cricket Committee met and reached two significant decisions: to accept a block grant of £6,500 from the Gillette Razor Company, sponsors of the new one-day knockout competition due to start the following season; and to recommend the abolition of the amateur status, so that henceforth all players would be known as cricketers. 'Cricket Breaks with the Past' was the headline in *The Times* the next morning, and most commentators accepted the decision as inevitable. A dissenter was Swanton: confessing himself to be 'a crusted reactionary', he rested his case on the captaincy question, arguing that 'the essence of leadership is independence' and that by definition a professional could not provide that quality. The most illustrious of professionals, Sir Jack Hobbs, did not disagree:

> It is sad to see the passing of the amateurs, because it signals the end of an era in cricket. They were a great asset to the game, much appreciated by all of us because they were able to come in and play freely, whereas many professionals did not feel they could take chances.

On 30 January 1963 Sir Pelham Warner, the patron saint of a condemned fixture, died. The following day the MCC committee confirmed without dissent the abolition of the amateur status in first-class cricket. A brave new world was dawning and WG was left for all time as the only amateur to have taken over two and a half thousand wickets or (if one excludes Hammond) scored over forty thousand runs.

All twenty-two participants in his jubilee match were dead, yet for a dozen more years there lived on the man who had fielded so capably for both Gentlemen and Players. Wilfred Rhodes died near his home in Dorset on 8 July 1973 at the age of ninety-five, almost three-quarters of a century after those days of toil. Perhaps the greatest of all Yorkshire's professionals, certainly the wisest, he had never had any time for the ethical, 'It's not cricket' approach so often wheeled out by defenders of the two-class system. He knew it was only a game – the best of games, to be played hard and fairly – but still only a game. And one old man, if confronted with that proposition, would have stroked his beard thoughtfully and, in his inarticulate way, agreed.

Author's Note

The text of *WG's Birthday Party*, first published in 1990, remains essentially unchanged in this new edition. I have, however, learned much about WG from reading Simon Rae's fine biography, published in 1998 to mark the 150th anniversary of his birth. It is the most acute study yet of a remarkable man, someone who did not mind losing but could not bear being crossed. This re-issue of my own, much less ambitious study will serve, I hope, as an additional reminder of Grace's imperishable uniqueness as 'The Great Cricketer'.

JANUARY 2010

Note on the Author

David Kynaston was born in Aldershot in 1951. He has been a professional historian since 1973 and has written eighteen books, including *The City of London* (1994–2001), a widely acclaimed four-volume history. He is the author of *Austerity Britain 1945–51* and *Family Britain 1951–57*, the first two titles in a series of books covering the history of post-war Britain (1945-1979) under the collective title 'Tales of a New Jerusalem'. His other two cricket books are *Bobby Abel, Professional Batsman* and *Archie's Last Stand: MCC in New Zealand 1922–23*. He is currently a visiting professor at Kingston University.

Also available by David Kynaston

Austerity Britain, 1945–1951

'The book is a marvel . . . the fullest, deepest and most balanced history of our times'
Sunday Telegraph

Coursing through *Austerity Britain* is an astonishing variety of voices – vivid, unselfconscious, and unaware of what the future holds. A Chingford housewife endures the tribulations of rationing; a retired schoolteacher observes during a royal visit how well-fed the Queen looks; a pernickety civil servant in Bristol is oblivious to anyone's troubles but his own. An array of working-class witnesses describe how life in post-war Britain is, with little regard for liberal niceties or the feelings of their 'betters'.

Many of these voices will stay with the reader in future volumes, jostling alongside well-known figures like John Arlott (here making his first radio broadcast, still in police uniform), Glenda Jackson (taking the 11+) and Doris Lessing, newly arrived from Africa, struck by the levelling poverty of postwar Britain. David Kynaston weaves a sophisticated narrative of how the victorious 1945 Labour government shaped the political, economic and social landscape for the next three decades. Deeply researched, often amusing and always intensely entertaining and readable, the first volume of David Kynaston's ambitious history offers an entirely fresh perspective on Britain during those six momentous years.

'This is a classic; buy at least three copies – one for yourself and two to give to friends and family'
John Charmley, *Guardian*

'A wonderfully illuminating picture of the way we were'
Roy Hattersley, The Times

ISBN: 9780747599234 / **Paperback** / £9.99

Family Britain, 1951–1957

'I could quote forever from this magnificent book.
Professor Kynaston is the most entertaining historian alive'
Philip Hensher, *Spectator*

Family Britain brilliantly continues David Kynaston's groundbreaking history
of post-war Britain with a vivid portrait of the 1950s, a time when Britain was
starting to move away from the hardships of austerity. Great national events
jostle alongside everything that gave 1950s Britain its distinctive flavor from
Butlin's holiday camps, Kenwood food mixers and *Hancock's Half-Hour* to Ekco
television sets, skiffle and teddy boys. An astonishing array of vivid, intimate and
unselfconscious voices drive the narrative, punctuated by the appearance of such
well-known figures as Doris Lessing (joining and later leaving the Communist
Party), John Arlott (sticking up on *Any Questions?* for the rights of homosexuals)
and *Tiger*'s Roy of the Rovers (making his debut for Melchester). *Family Britain*
offers an unrivalled perspective on Britain during seven momentous years.

'An outstanding history evokes Fifties' Britain in all its conservatism, idealism and
lost innocence . . . Plenty of historians have written about it before. But none have
captured it better or with more human sympathy than David Kynaston, in this deeply
researched, richly detailed and very moving book. ★★★★★' *Daily Telegraph*

'Evocative and hugely appealing . . . On almost every page
there is an arresting detail, statistic or quotation' *Sunday Times*

ISBN: 9781408800836 / **Paperback** / £10.99

Order by phone: +44 (0) 1256 302 699
By email: direct@macmillan.co.uk
Delivery is usually 3–5 working days.
Postage and packaging will be charged.
Online: www.bloomsbury.com/bookshop
Free postage and packaging for orders over £20.
Prices and availability subject to change without notice

www.bloomsbury.com/davidkynaston